10 YEARS THAT SHOOK THE WORLD

10 YEARS THAT SHOOK THE WORLD

A Timeline of Events from 2001

LORETTA NAPOLEONI

SEVEN STORIES PRESS
New York

Seven Stories Press
140 Watts Street
New York, NY 10013
www.sevenstories.com

College professors may order examination copies of Seven Stories Press titles for a
free six-month trial period. To order, visit http://www.sevenstories.com/textbook or
send a fax on school letterhead to (212) 226-1411.

Book design by EPL

Napoleoni, Loretta.
 10 years that shook the world : a timeline of events from 2001 / Loretta Napoleoni.
-- Seven stories press 1st ed.
     p. cm.
 Includes bibliographical references.
 ISBN 978-1-60980-413-8 (pbk.)
 1. History, Modern--21st century--Chronology. 2. Civilization, Modern--21st
century--Chronology. 3. September 11 Terrorist Attacks, 2001--Influence. I. Title.
II. Title: Ten years that shook the world.
 D862.N37 2011
 909.83'11--dc23

                              2011035620

Printed in the United States

9 8 7 6 5 4 3 2 1

Table of Contents

Preface

THIS BOOKLET WAS ORIGINALLY intended for young people, those who were children or adolescents on September 11, 2001, and grew by research and writing to be a book for everybody. The aim is to show how the decade that began in 2001 has profoundly changed the world, setting in motion what Steve Jobs calls "digital lifestyle."

The attacks of September 11, 2001, are considered to have been the main event, but the changes of that decade go far beyond the menace of terrorism and the War on Terror. The technological revolution triggered by Apple, the wide use of the web, the advent of social media, and stem cell research are just some of the innovations that brought about a new Enlightenment. The War on Terror and its strong rhetoric hid these phenomena. The purpose of this booklet is to show the true patterns of change—those innovations that will influence coming decades.

While politicians were chasing the ghosts of al-Qaeda, the economy was spinning out of control, leading us to the 2008 financial crisis and the ensuing recession. Emerging markets, where the technological revolution brought modernity at a very fast pace, were the true winners of the decade. In the space of 10 years, the BRIC countries (Brazil, Russia, India, and China) became major players in the world economy, the euro reached the brink of collapse, and United States economic predominance continued its decline.

The demographic explosion is eroding the environment and putting pressure on natural resources. We cannot live as we have done until today. This is the decade in which these problems, and our responses to them, are finally pushing us towards real political, economic, and environmental change.

A youth revolution empowered by social media used the web to reject obsolete values, demanding a pivotal role in a society where young people were only consumers. From the pop economy to the Arab revolt, the world is beginning a new chapter in modern history. Fifty years from now, people will look at this decade as a major milestone in human progress.

This booklet is written in short bursts of information, similar to 140-character tweets. This is the modern narrative, the one used by many young people, and it reflects the rapid pace of change and communication in this modern world. More than a timeline, *10 Years That Shook the World* tells the tale of an extraordinary decade. Within each year, events are presented not in a strict chronology but more as we might remember them, often with the most significant events recalled first. Thus the main topics—politics, economics, people, technology, and the environment—cross over constantly, showing how they are all interlinked and how globalization poses a phenomenal challenge to our world.

—LN, August 2011

Acknowledgments

THIS BOOK NEVER WOULD have happened without Björn Axelsson and Matteo Ballero, my research assistants. I owe this book to them.

To them goes not only my gratitude but also my admiration for piecing together such a unique story of a decade nobody will ever forget.

Thank you also to my stepson Andrew Gerson for editing this book, and to my sons Julian and Alexander for reading it and suggesting additional tweets.

2001
At a Glance

World gross domestic product (GDP): $32.009tn
  US: $10.234tn
  Japan: $4.095tn
  Germany: $1.891tn

World population: 6.162bn

Natural disasters:
  12,000 die in an earthquake in India
  800 die in an earthquake in El Salvador

US federal debt: $5.807tn
US unemployment: 4.74%

Average oil price: $23 per barrel
Annual food price index (2002–2004=100): 93.3

World military spending: $772bn
  US: $281.4bn
  Russia: $43.9bn
  France: $40.4bn
US share of total military spending: 36.5%

Time magazine person of the year: Rudolph Giuliani

Nobel Peace Prize winners: United Nations and Kofi Annan "for their work for a better organized and more peaceful world."

Introduction

The deadliest terrorist attack on US soil to date changes the world at the outset of the new millennium. From this day forward, the global movement against exploitative globalization that had previously dominated the world agenda finds itself taking a backseat to the war on terror.

US President George W. Bush had campaigned on an isolationist platform in foreign policy, saying, "If we don't stop extending our troops all around the world in nation-building missions, then we're going to have a serious problem coming down the road. And I'm going to prevent that."

The newly inaugurated president now finds himself at the center of world politics, with every nation watching for his reaction.

In the midst of the political turmoil, Apple launches the iPod and iTunes; the music world will never be the same.

Three months after the execution of Timothy McVeigh for the bombing of the Oklahoma City federal building, where 168 people died, comes 9/11.

19 al-Qaeda hijackers fly two commercial flights into the World Trade Center and another into the Pentagon.

A fourth plane, United Airlines 93, heading for the White House, crashes near Pittsburgh, PA, possibly because passengers overwhelm the terrorists.

A bewildered international media broadcasts the New York attack live; the world watches in horror as burning people jump to their deaths from the Twin Towers.

New York Mayor Rudy Giuliani gets trapped by smoke and debris for 20 minutes in a building near the World Trade Center.

Giuliani closes the New York Stock Exchange, which will remain shut for four days, and President George W. Bush tells Americans to go home, stay home, and wait.

For a few days life in the US comes to a halt. The impact is devastating for the already weak US economy.

In March, financial markets had already fully grasped the consequences of the dot-com crash, described by the *Guardian* as "a slaughter of dot-com ventures."

The 2000 slowdown of the US manufacturing sector that ended the dot-com boom spreads throughout the US economy in 2001.

As all economic indicators point toward a possible recession, the Fed cuts interest rates to reboot the economy.

The Fed will keep cutting rates throughout the decade.

After 9/11, resumed trading on Wall Street takes place in a climate of great uncertainty and fear.

On the first day of trading the market plunges to 8,920 on the Dow Jones Index (7.1% from the closing on 9/10).

Across the dealing rooms of the global village echo the eerie words of Saudi-born Osama bin Laden, the man behind the 9/11 attack: "We will bleed the American economy to death."

While the tragedy unfolds, it becomes clear that together with the Dow Jones, Moody's rating, Coca-Cola, and CNN, terrorism has become a global phenomenon.

The apocalyptic images of the collapse of the Twin Towers fuel a messianic, religious response from a US administration rich in born-again Christians.

"Thousands of lives have been suddenly ended by evil," says Bush, describing Osama bin Laden and al-Qaeda and encouraging Americans to pray.

Born from the mujahedin army in the late 1980s, al-Qaeda is its ragged vanguard, which promotes Islamic fundamentalism in the Muslim world.

Controlled by bin Laden and by the Egyptian doctor al Zawahiri, in the late 1990s al-Qaeda becomes the first transnational terrorist organization.

Facing two foes, the near enemy of corrupt oligarchic Muslim elites and the far away enemy of the US which backs them, al-Qaeda focuses on the latter.

In 1998 bin Laden ordered the bombing of the US embassies in Kenya and Tanzania; in 2000 the attack against the *USS Cole* in Yemen.

After residing for several years in Sudan, bin Laden moves to Afghanistan, where he runs terrorist camps under the protection of its rulers, the Taliban.

Mullah Omar, the spiritual leader of the Taliban, shares with al-Qaeda a strong religious commitment to a deeply conservative interpretation of Islam.

In August, the Federal Emergency Management Agency (FEMA) warns officials that the three most likely disasters to hit the US are: a hurricane striking New Orleans, a massive earthquake in San Francisco, and a terrorist attack on New York City.

On September 14 the world stands still for three silent minutes in honor of the victims while contemplating the forthcoming battle between "good and evil."

Gladiator wins most of the Oscars and becomes the one of the most popular films of the year, reinforcing the images of a clash between good and evil.

Al-Qaeda's propaganda couples an archaic vision of Islam with a technological knowledge of viral marketing.

This explosive mix spreads al-Qaeda's apocalyptic message worldwide.

9/11 unleashes a make-believe clash between two cultures: West and East; two religions: Christianity and Islam; two worlds: present and past.

Prof. Huntington's *Clash of Civilizations* provides the ideological framework for Bush's crusade: the "war on terror."

"Either you are with us, or you are with the terrorists," says the US president, forcing the world to revert to the familiar Cold War dichotomy now dressed in religious clothes.

In New York, Rudolph Giuliani becomes the beacon of strength and hope against the new enemy for New Yorkers, emotionally overwhelmed by the tragedy.

"I want the people of New York to be an example to the rest of the country, and the rest of the world, that terrorism can't stop us," proclaims Giuliani.

On the web, anti-American messages from al-Qaeda's followers start to surface, encouraging Muslims to attack America and American interests abroad.

The rise of Napster enables online file sharing of music, reaching 26.4m users in February. The music industry, both amazed and afraid of its success, begins legal proceedings.

A US Court of Appeals confirms a district court ruling that Napster has to shut down due to copyright infringements. But the music revolution has begun!

It will open the way toward major changes in telecommunications.

Steve Jobs launches the new Mac OS X, Apple's operating system that rivals Microsoft, and attempts to reach world supremacy.

Jobs defines Apple's long-term vision as the advent of a "digital lifestyle."

The iPod, Apple's version of a portable media player, hits the market in October 2001; in 10 years it would sell 297m units worldwide.

9/11 ends the anemic US economic recovery.

In September, US retail sales drop 2.4%, the largest fall in nine years. October sees the highest jump in unemployment in 21 years, with 415,000 people losing their jobs.

The transportation and insurance industries are badly hit, spreading bankruptcy across the blue-chip sector.

The highly conservative PATRIOT Act, which limits US liberties, also blocks the entry of terror and dirty money into the US.

As an anti-money laundering legislation, it gives the US monetary authority the power to monitor all US dollar transactions in the world.

Following the introduction of the PATRIOT Act, Muslim investors repatriate $900bn dollars held in US portfolios for fear of harassment from the US government.

Money laundering in the US becomes problematic and migrates to Europe.

New alliances between Latin American narcos and the European mafia blossom, opening new drug routes from South America to Europe via western Africa.

The international banking community does not like the PATRIOT Act and advises clients to switch from dollar to euro investments.

The dollar value vis-à-vis the euro starts to fall as both legitimate and illegal businesses switch to the euro.

Antiterrorist legislation impacts the already bruised antiglobalization movement born in Seattle in 1999 during the WTO meeting.

At the 27th G8 Summit in Genoa, world leaders gather to discuss poverty reduction mechanisms.

The antiglobalization movement defines the G8 as an illegitimate attempt by eight countries to use their economic power to set rules for the entire world.

The Italian government suspends the Schengen Agreement, which allows freedom of movement inside the EU, and seals the Red Zone, where the summit takes place.

The G8 lasts three days. A crowd of 200,000 NO-GLOBAL demonstrators overshadows the world leaders.

During the G8, 329 protestors are arrested; 400 more are injured, together with 100 policemen.

The dark side of globalization fuels a clash between Western leaders and youth movements. Years later it will resurface in Europe when unemployed youth will demand jobs.

The environment is one of the main topics of this clash.

11 leading scientists of the US National Academy of Sciences say that the atmosphere is getting warmer due to human activity.

Tropical Storm Allison produces 36 inches of rain in Houston, Texas, killing 22 and causing more than $5bn of damage overall.

Bush refuses to ratify the Kyoto Protocol, which limits carbon emissions.

Wikipedia, an online interactive encyclopedia, is launched on the Internet. It will become the voice of the people.

In October, the US passes an unsuccessful $100bn economic stimulus package to revive the agonizing economy. Then comes the anthrax scare.

Spending freezes and fear spreads as media outlets and government officials receive letters that contain deadly anthrax spores. Five people die.

"You cannot stop us. We have this Anthrax. You die now. Are you afraid?" reads the letters that spread the threat of biological terrorism linked to 9/11.

The politics of fear start to take shape: in the collective imagination, tomorrow will bring more menace than today.

To date, authorities have not determined the origin of the letters, nor have they unraveled the anthrax mystery.

Bush directs anguish toward Iraq: "Facing clear evidence of peril, we cannot wait for the final proof, the smoking gun that could come in the form of a mushroom cloud."

On October 7, to find and punish terrorists or "those harboring terrorists," the US and an international coalition attack Afghanistan.

"We are supported by the collective will of the world," Bush says. About 40 nations come on board in the nascent antiterror coalition. The war on terror has begun.

Italy, which had just elected media magnate Silvio Berlusconi prime minister, joins the coalition. Berlusconi is one of the 50 richest men in the world.

Under US pressure, Pakistan becomes the United States' chief ally in the war on terror.

General Pervez Musharraf, who had come to power during a military coup in 1999, appoints himself president of Pakistan.

President Bush ends sanctions on Pakistan for developing nuclear power in 1998, reschedules its debt, and helps Musharraf consolidate his power.

In spite of their improving relationship, China and the US get tangled in a diplomatic incident when a US spy plane and a Chinese jet collide.

In the US, the cloning of human embryos for stem cell research, considered the best hope for finding cures for Alzheimer's and Parkinson's, sparks a violent debate.

The use of embryonic stem cell research drives the ire of pro-life, antiabortion, and religious groups who believe the embryo has a life of its own.

Bush allows funding for research using only existing stem cell lines, "where the decision on life and death has already been made."

Harry Potter and the Sorcerer's Stone opens in 8,200 US theaters, about 1/4 of all those available, earning an unprecedented $93.5m in one weekend.

In November, an American Airlines plane crashes in Queens, New York, killing all 255 people on board. People fear another terrorist attack.

The menace of terrorism sparks a renewed interest in the stalled Middle East peace process. In 2001 alone, 800 people die in the Israeli-Palestinian conflict.

Violence erupts again in Israel when three suicide bombers attack Jerusalem and the port city of Haifa, killing 25 Israelis.

Ariel Sharon's newly elected Israeli government bombs targets in the West Bank and Gaza in retaliation for the Jerusalem and Haifa suicide attack.

Former Serbian leader Slobodan Milosevic, on trial in The Hague for genocide and crimes against humanity during the civil war in the former Yugoslavia, rejects the authority of the Human Rights Court.

The Irish Republican Army (IRA) declares that it has begun dismantling its arms arsenal as agreed in the peace process with the UK government.

In December, to counteract rising unemployment and revive consumer spending, the Fed cuts interest rates for a record 11th time in 2001.

Enron files for Chapter 11 bankruptcy protection five days after Dynegy, the Texan energy company, cancels an $8.4bn buyout bid.

The Taliban regime collapses and coalition forces nominate Hamid Karzai, the US-backed candidate, to head the transitional government in Afghanistan.

The shoe bomber, Richard Reid, is arrested when he fails to detonate his shoes on an Air France flight from Paris to Miami.

2002
At a Glance

World GDP: $33.2tn
   US: $10.6tn
   Japan: $3.9tn
   Germany: $2tn

World population: 6.238bn

Natural disasters:
   147 people die, about 500,000 are evacuated from Mount Nyiragongo eruption
   Dozens of people die, billions of dollars of damage caused by floods in Central Europe
   Approximately 1,000 people die in an earthquake in Afghanistan

US federal debt: $6.228tn
US unemployment: 5.78%

Average oil price: $22.81 per barrel
Annual food price index (2002–2004=100): 89.9

World military spending: $784bn
   US: $335.7bn
   Japan: $46.7bn
   UK: $36.0bn
US share of total military spending: 43%

Time magazine people of the year: Whistleblowers Sherron Watkins of Enron, Coleen Rowley of the FBI, and Cynthia Cooper of WorldCom

Nobel Peace Prize winner: Jimmy Carter "for his decades of untiring effort to find peaceful solutions to international conflicts, to advance democracy and human rights, and to promote economic and social development."

Introduction

With the development of the Internet came business expectations: vast amounts of money are invested in online businesses that show little profit. Baby millionaires, 20-something-year-olds with businesses worth millions of dollars throwing lavish parties, are characteristic of the the dot-com bubble era.

The Internet, it is predicted, will change the laws of economics, replacing them with "the New Economy." Sadly, age-old economic rules prove accurate yet again as the dot-com bubble falls apart, soon to be followed by the spectacular bankruptcies of Enron and WorldCom.

A US Congressional committee publishes a memo in which Sherron Watkins, vice president of Corporate Development at Enron, denounces accounting fraud at the US energy giant.

The memo is addressed to Kenneth Lay, Enron's founder. Soon afterwards, the Enron scandal erupts.

The company goes bankrupt, leading to the dissolution of Arthur Andersen, one of the largest audit and accountancy partnerships in the world.

In addition to being the largest bankruptcy reorganization in American history at the time, Enron Corporation becomes the biggest audit failure.

A few months later, AOL Time Warner loses $54bn from the burst of the dot-com bubble.

In 2000, AOL Time Warner was valued at $181bn; by 2002 the company's credit worthiness had plummeted to $101bn.

The dot-com crisis unveils unethical behaviors among major corporations' CEOs who hide lackluster financial reports while profiting personally from stock sales.

Among the first to resign is Bernie Ebbers, CEO of WorldCom, the world's largest Internet network, which employs 60,000 people in 65 countries.

Ebbers had taken $366m in personal loans from WorldCom while the company had an outstanding $41bn debt.

Cynthia Cooper, a WorldCom employee, discovers that operating costs have been entered as capital expenditures on the company's balance sheet, thus inflating profits.

A $4bn hole in WorldCom finances emerges, triggering the firing of WorldCom CFO Scott Sullivan and another 17,000 workers in just one week.

WorldCom files for Chapter 11 of the bankruptcy code, causing the largest bankruptcy in US history ($107bn), overtaken only in 2008 by the collapse of Lehman Brothers.

America gets hit by a wave of embarrassing corporate scandals: Enron, Arthur Andersen, Merrill Lynch, WorldCom, Johnson & Johnson, Global Crossing, Citigroup, and Kmart.

Well-known and well-respected American businesses and celebrities come under fire.

Home decorating maven Martha Stewart faces allegations of insider trading for selling 4,000 shares of ImClone stock shortly before the stock's value plummeted.

Investors sue investment banks that have advised them to buy shares of high-tech companies when they knew these were poor investments.

Major investment banks settle the cases and pay out a total of $1.4bn in damages.

Though the recession triggered by 9/11 is short-lived, corporate scandals, stock market turmoil, and the prospect of more terror attacks and war beset the economy.

In a bid to stimulate the economy, the Federal Reserve slashes interest rates to a 40-year low.

Federal Chairman Alan Greenspan says the economy has hit a "soft patch," but claims he is hopeful of avoiding another recession.

The governor of California, Gray Davis, announces that the state will face a record budget deficit of $35bn, roughly double the figure reported during his reelection campaign one month earlier.

Argentina defaults on an $805m World Bank payment.

China bans Google in an attempt to limit Chinese access to Western media. However, a month later it lifts the ban, allowing Chinese Internet users to surf the net via Google.

Trent Lott, a US Republican senator and majority leader in the Senate, resigns after bloggers reveal his racist comments during a private party.

Lott said that he would have voted for Thurmond, who in 1948 ran for president as a segregationist, and that if others had done so, "We wouldn't have had all these problems over all these years."

For the infant blogosphere, Lott's resignation is a major victory over the traditional media that had completely missed the story.

The first public version of the web browser Mozilla Firefox ("Phoenix 0.1") is released.

The Salt Lake City Olympic Games open full of doubts, with heightened security to protect against terror attacks.

The games' organizers come under intense scrutiny amid reports of bribery and overindulgence. Storms erupt over alleged vote-rigging in figure skating and controversial calls in speed skating.

The events end peacefully 17 days later, making this Winter Olympics one of the best run, if most controversial, in history.

In Europe, the euro finally becomes a reality when 12 European countries adopt the single currency, uniting a continent long divided by different languages, cultures, and traditions.

Used as an electronic currency since 1999, the euro soon becomes an alternative to the US dollar.

Weeks before the euro is launched, troops are deployed to help move 50bn euro coins, weighing almost 240,000 tons, and 15bn banknotes from 15 printing presses across the EU.

After a two-month transition period, old currencies like the German mark, French franc, Italian lira, and Portuguese escudo cease to be legal tender in these countries.

President Bush casts Iraq as part of an "axis of evil" together with Iran and North Korea; the war of words continues to escalate in subsequent months.

The White House calls for regime change and accuses Iraqi leader Saddam Hussein of developing chemical, biological, and nuclear weapons.

Baghdad derides members of the Bush administration as Israeli propagandists and warmongers bent on destroying their country.

Under the umbrella of the war on terror, Vladimir Putin and Ariel Sharon launch military campaigns against the Chechnyan rebels and the Palestinian people respectively.

In Pakistan a Jihadist group kidnaps and murders Daniel Pearl, a journalist from the *Wall Street Journal* who was researching a story about the shoe bomber Richard Reid.

The US administration takes prisoners from Afghanistan and brings them to the US military base in Guantánamo, Cuba.

Chained and caged, men in orange jumpsuits begin filling front pages and TV screens.

Secretary of Defense Donald Rumsfeld scribbles on a memo: "I stand for 8–10 hours a day. Why is standing [by prisoners] limited to 4 hours?" The comment is seen as an authorization of unconventional interrogation methods.

"American Taliban" John Walker Lindh returns to the United States under the custody of the Federal Bureau of Investigation and stands trial in a US court.

Distancing itself from the international community, the US refuses to ratify the International Criminal Court at The Hague.

Hamid Karzai, widely seen as a puppet of the Americans, becomes the first (interim) president of democratic Afghanistan. However, the country continues to be beset by adversarial warlords while its economy is ravaged by decades of war.

12 months after the invasion of Afghanistan, coalition forces continue to fight pockets of al-Qaeda and Taliban fighters, trying to bring order to a volatile nation.

The new American national security strategy claims to focus on human rights. In a move that jettisons international law, the new US policy is to interfere wherever there are human rights violations, discarding the age old respect for sovereignty of nations.

This policy change enables the idea of a preemptive strike, i.e., an attack to prevent being attacked. The policy is used as a justification for a war of aggression.

Bush stresses that all means are allowed in the war on terror, including torture.

The preemptive strike doctrine becomes the ideological justification for an attack against Saddam Hussein, who, according to Bush and Blair, could supply nuclear warheads to Osama bin Laden.

The idea of a coming military conflict with Iraq is publicized in the US right after Labor Day, because "from a marketing point of view, you don't introduce new products in August," explains White House Chief of Staff Andrew Card.

Scott Ritter, former UN weapons inspector in Iraq, strongly dismisses the claim that Iraq possesses or could produce weapons of mass destruction (WMD) on any meaningful scale.

There were weapons inspectors in Iraq in the 1990s, but they were forced to leave after a squabble between the Iraqi government and the UN over CIA agents infiltrating the weapons inspectors' group.

Bush's Secretary of State, Colin Powell, seeks a resolution from the UN Security Council to grant inspectors unconditional access to Iraq and the right to use force if Saddam Hussein fails to comply.

In September, Tony Blair releases an intelligence dossier stating the case for military intervention in Iraq.

The dossier claims that Saddam Hussein "has existing and active military plans for the use of chemical and biological weapons, which could be activated within 45 minutes."

A report would later prove that the 45-minute claim was "officially false." On the eve of the Iraq invasion in 2003, Tony Blair will not mention the 45-minute claim in his war speech.

However, the 45-minute claim becomes an influential part of the political rhetoric and of the media narrative.

An anonymous British defense analyst is the first to express doubt about the 45-minute claim.

The analyst tells BBC correspondent Andrew Gilligan that the claim is a "classic example" of how the war dossier had been "sexed up."

The UK government soon discovers the name of the defense analyst, Professor David Kelly, and leaks his identity to the press.

Under exceptional pressure from the media, Kelly tries to hide. Eventually he is found dead in the woods near his home.

Did Kelly really commit suicide? The *Daily Telegraph* prints the word suicide in quotation marks, suggesting he may have been murdered. His post-mortem report is classified until 2010; upon release it says he died of self-inflicted wounds.

The preemptive strike doctrine coupled with Blair's sexed-up war dossier triggers a worldwide antiwar protest. 150,000 people gather in London, chanting, "Tony Blair, shame, shame, no more killing in my name."

Up until the invasion of Iraq in March 2003, antiwar demonstrators will fill the streets and squares of the world protesting against the war.

In November, half a million people participate in the first European Social Forum in Florence, Italy, under the slogan: "Against war, racism, and neo-liberalism," referencing Bush's war against Iraq.

In a letter to the United Nations, Saddam Hussein writes, "In targeting Iraq, America is acting for the Zionists who are killing the heroic people of Palestine, destroying their properties, murdering their children, and working to impose domination on the whole world."

Bush's reply comes in a pro-war speech at the UN that leads to a resolution calling for the inspectors' return, pledging "serious consequences" if Iraq does not cooperate.

Eventually the weapon inspections team headed by Swedish diplomat Hans Blix returns to Iraq in search for chemical, biological, and nuclear weapons.

At the American Music Awards, Michael Jackson wins Artist of the Century.

Allegations of illicit sex and molestation rock the Roman Catholic Church when the *Boston Globe* reveals that dozens of Catholic priests have abused children.

Many victims step forward, unveiling a massive cover-up operation within the Catholic Church that has gone on for years.

Though the Boston Archdiocese is at the epicenter, the crisis affects parishes from Los Angeles to New York and catches the attention of future Pope Benedict XVI, who does his best to cover it up.

Church officials are accused of moving priests who sexually abused children and teenagers to different parishes, without warning parishioners or disclosing the reason for the transfers.

After months of pressure, Cardinal Bernard Law, Archbishop of the Boston Archdiocese, resigns over allegations that he did not take stronger action to deal with the problems.

The scandal leaves many Catholics angry and disillusioned.

British police arrest 36 people in what becomes known as "Operation Ore," the first to target people who trade child pornography on the Internet.

The Netherlands becomes the first nation in the world to legalize euthanasia.

The funeral of Queen Elizabeth The Queen Mother draws large crowds at Westminster Abbey, London.

Citizens of Switzerland narrowly vote in favor of their country becoming a member of the United Nations.

Former US President Jimmy Carter visits Cuba to meet Fidel Castro and becomes the first president of the United States to set foot on the island since Castro's 1959 revolution.

Denzel Washington and Halle Berry make Hollywood history by becoming the second and third African Americans to win best acting honors in the Oscars' 74-year history.

Washington, who won for playing a rogue cop in *Training Day*, pays tribute in his victory speech to Sidney Poitier, the only previous African American best actor winner.

An emotional Berry, winning for her role in *Monster's Ball*, dedicates her award to "every nameless, faceless woman of color who now has a chance because this door tonight has been opened."

Michael Moore's documentary *Bowling for Columbine* fills movie theaters. The movie gives fuel to the debate about the American right to bear arms.

In April, Jean-Marie Le Pen, the far-right French politician, comes second in the first round of France's presidential election.

Le Pen takes 17% of the vote, eliminating Lionel Jospin, the Socialist prime minister, who takes only 16%.

Stunned by the result, Jospin withdraws his bid and throws his support behind President Jacques Chirac, who wins the final round in a landslide.

Le Pen's party, the National Front, does not win a single seat in parliament.

In the US, Nancy Pelosi is elected leader of the Democrats in the House of Representatives. She is the first woman to achieve such a position.

After 19 months of house arrest, Aung San Suu Kyi, the Burmese opposition leader and 1991 winner of the Nobel Peace Prize, is freed. She will be arrested again one year later.

In her first public speech, Suu Kyi promises to "make sure democracy comes to Burma."

The military junta declares that she can travel freely within the country, facing no restrictions on her political activities.

NASA's Mars Odyssey begins its mapping mission of Mars, which leads to the discovery of hydrogen trapped in big sheets of ice beneath the planet's surface.

"It really just blew us away when we looked at it," scientist William Boynton tells the *LA Times*. The presence of prehistoric hydrogen hints at the possibility of water, and perhaps even life on Mars.

As news stories surface about North Korea's nuclear program, Bush opts for a diplomatic solution.

In what is later dubbed the "Passover Massacre," a suicide bomber kills 30 people in Netanya, Israel.

In another attack, a Palestinian suicide bomber kills 7 and injures 104 at the Mahane Yehuda Market in Jerusalem.

The 38-day stand-off in the Church of the Nativity in Bethlehem comes to an end when the Palestinians inside agree to have 13 suspected militants among them deported to different countries.

In response to the wave of suicide attacks, Israel begins the construction of a tall, concrete wall around Palestinian territories. Across the world, parallels are made with the Berlin Wall in the 1960s.

Chechen rebels take 763 hostages and hold them for three days in a Moscow theater. Before storming the theater, police release an unknown gas, killing 116 people.

For three weeks in October, John Allen Muhammad, a Gulf War veteran, spreads fear in the Washington DC area, killing 10 people and injuring many others before being arrested with his accomplice, John Lee Malvo, 17, from Jamaica.

Authorities later link the pair to earlier shootings in Atlanta, Georgia; Montgomery, Alabama; and Baton Rouge, Louisiana.

On October 12, the bloodiest terror attack of the year occurs in Bali, Indonesia.

More than 180 people, about half of them Australians, die after a van laden with explosives and another, smaller bomb explode outside a packed nightclub.

Al-Qaeda operatives take credit for the Bali attacks. Osama bin Laden is believed to have funded the bombing.

During the year, al-Qaeda's followers stage attacks on a Tunisian synagogue, a French oil tanker off Yemen, and an Israeli-owned airliner and hotel in Kenya.

President Bush creates the Department of Homeland Security to conduct the US' "titanic struggle against terrorism." Employing 170,000 persons, it's second only to the Pentagon in size.

This move puts into motion the largest reorganization of the US Federal Government in more than half a century.

In New York on the first anniversary of 9/11, a moment of silence at Ground Zero becomes a powerful memorial commemorating the terror attacks, in stark contrast to the noises of chaos and horror of the year before.

Thousands attend vigils and concerts and even form a human chain to remember 9/11 and the victims of the atrocities after 12 months of grief.

At the end of the summer, Bush declines to attend the World Summit on Sustainable Development in Johannesburg, although at the last moment Colin Powell makes an appearance.

Without US backing, agreements made at the summit are functionally meaningless.

Commentators echo Bush Sr.'s comment at the Rio Earth Summit 10 years earlier: "The American way of life is not negotiable."

In November, the oil tanker *Prestige* sinks off the coast of Spain and Portugal, producing the worst environmental disaster ever sustained by these countries.

Fierce winds, driving downpours, and severe flooding wreak havoc in Europe, causing dozens of deaths and billions of dollars of damage.

From Spain to Ukraine, the continent's worst flooding in decades turns rivers and streets into deadly torrents.

Some areas receive a month's worth of rain in just 24 hours, with Austria recording its worst rains in more than 100 years.

The resulting floodwaters wash away homes, buildings, and bridges; destroy telephone and electricity lines; submerge railway tracks; and damage crops.

Lucio Gutiérrez wins the presidential election in Ecuador, following his campaign to end corruption and reverse neoliberal reforms. His largest constituency is made up of the landless, the poor, and the indigenous people.

2003
At a Glance

World GDP: $37.4tn
   US: $11tn
   Japan: $4.2tn
   Germany: $2.4tn

World population: 6.315bn

Natural disasters:
   Over 2,000 people die in an earthquake in Algeria
   Over 25,000 people die in an earthquake in Iran

US federal debt: $6.783bn
US unemployment: 6%

Average oil price: $27.69 per barrel
Annual food price index (2002–2004=100): 97.7

World military spending: $879bn
   US: $417.4bn
   Japan: $46.9bn
   UK: $37.1bn
US share of total military spending: 47.5%

Time magazine person of the year: the American soldier

Nobel Peace Prize winner: Shirin Ebadi "for her efforts for democracy and human rights. She has focused especially on the struggle for the rights of women and children."

Introduction

The invasion of Iraq starts after a long build-up of forged evidence and wishful thinking. US Vice President Dick Cheney is convinced that the troops will be greeted as liberators.

The international political system breaks down with the war on Iraq, as coalition forces fail to win UN approval for a preemptive strike against Saddam Hussein. The Bush administration attempts to introduce a new world order centered around US supremacy and advances without the approval of the world's largest intergovernmental body.

Google becomes the largest search engine, overtaking Yahoo!. Skype is launched, removing the barriers to long-distance communication.

US Secretary of State Colin Powell addresses the UN Security Council, making the case for military intervention in Iraq, and urges the Council to back Washington and London in their pursuit of Saddam Hussein.

"I cannot tell you everything that we know. But what I can share with you . . . is deeply troubling. . . . Numerous human sources tell us that the Iraqis are moving, not just documents and hard drives, but weapons of mass destruction to keep them from being found by inspectors," Powell says.

"Every statement I make today is backed up by sources, solid sources. These are not assertions. What we're giving you are facts and conclusions based on solid intelligence," he adds.

"Leaving Saddam Hussein in possession of weapons of mass destruction for a few more months or years is not an option," he concludes, hinting that the US would intervene with or without UN backing.

Among the proofs of Saddam's alleged possession of WMD, the US presents to the world documentation of a sale of uranium from Niger.

Ambassador Joseph Wilson investigates the suspected uranium link between Niger and Iraq, but finds no evidence of Iraqi purchases of uranium.

But the US administration ignores Wilson's report.

Wilson then publishes an op-ed in the *New York Times*. In it he questions the Bush administration's proof of Iraq purchasing uranium for WMD.

The White House retaliates by leaking to the press the identity of Wilson's wife, CIA agent Valerie Plame, thereby ending her career and putting her life in danger.

Pulitzer Prize winner Judith Miller publishes a series of articles in the *New York Times* to support the Bush administration's case for waging war against Iraq.

She describes Saddam Hussein as very ambitious and capable of producing WMD.

Her sources, all originating from the White House, prove to be stunningly inaccurate. Miller resigns amid the *New York Times*' embarrassment.

"The International Atomic Energy Agency has concluded that these documents are in fact not authentic," says Mohamed ElBaradei, its director general, referring to US documents on the Iraq WMD program.

In the run-up to the invasion of Iraq, an estimated 11m people around the world take their rage to the streets to protest against the looming war. It is the largest protest in human history.

In London, 2m people meet in Hyde Park, where Ken Livingstone, mayor of London, says, "This war is solely about oil. George Bush has never given a damn about human rights."

The largest coordinated worldwide vigil takes place as part of the global protests against the Iraq war.

Donald Rumsfeld, the US defense secretary, dubs France, Germany, and other countries opposed to the coming war "Old Europe."

Condoleezza Rice, US national security advisor, is quoted as having advised President George W. Bush to "punish France, forgive Germany, and ignore Russia."

Former foreign secretary of Great Britain and current cabinet member Robin Cook resigns in opposition to the coming war in Iraq.

On expectation of military intervention in Iraq, the Dow Jones index falls below 8,000; economist Jeremy Siegal says markets are "nervous, anxious, and waiting."

The euro reaches a high of $1.18 for the first time since its introduction, as the dollar continues to weaken. The dollar remains weaker than the euro for the rest of the decade.

"American and coalition forces are in the early stages of military operations to disarm Iraq, to free its people, and to defend the world from grave danger," Bush says, marking the beginning of the second US-led Iraq War on March 19.

On March 20 American and British coalition forces begin invading Iraq without United Nations support and in defiance of world opinion.

In a taped message, Saddam Hussein denounces the US attack as "criminal" and Iraq's ambassador to the UN calls the invasion "a violation of international law."

It is believed that the war will be short. Both Dick Cheney and Donald Rumsfeld state that it will last "weeks, not months."

Within two weeks of the invasion, *USA Today* reports that US officials are now warning that it will not "be a quick and easy victory."

An independent organization called "Iraq Body Count" is formed. Its purpose is to do what the US says it will not: count the casualties of war.

The war in Iraq prompts the rise of a new form of media coverage: embedded journalism, which produces an often biased view of the conflict.

Coalition forces warn unembedded journalists that they cannot guarantee their safety.

A US missile strikes Al Jazeera's Baghdad offices. The same day a tank opens fire on the Palestine Hotel, the headquarters of a number of Western journalists.

Seymour Hersh, a Pulitzer Prize winning journalist, publishes a series of articles accusing the US of having forged reports about Iraq's WMD and listing those who would benefit from the war.

"Seymour Hersh is the closest thing American journalism has to a terrorist," says Richard Perle, chairman of the Defense Policy Board Advisory Committee and one of those named by Hersh in his articles.

The US and the UK amass nearly 300,000 troops in the Persian Gulf as the war proceeds quickly and victoriously for the invaders.

US forces reach Baghdad in two weeks. On April 9, a statue of Saddam Hussein is torn down. The protesters decapitate it and drag it through the streets, hitting it with their shoes.

Days later it transpires that the US military had staged the whole event.

Widespread looting follows the fall of Saddam Hussein. Despite international warnings, US forces choose not to protect the Baghdad Museum and other important sites.

The Iraqi museum's collections include some of the most precious objects from the dawn of human civilization. As a result, thousands of historical items are stolen.

Three of the Bush administration's most senior cultural advisors resign in protest.

The US disregard for Iraqi cultural treasures causes outrage throughout the world. Commentators note that the US forces are interested in protecting solely the Ministry of Oil.

Dressed as a pilot and standing on the aircraft carrier *USS Abraham Lincoln*, George W. Bush declares the "end of major combat" in Iraq. The banner over his head reads "Mission Accomplished."

In his address, Bush adds, "The war on terror continues," signaling that America is engaged in a long-term fight.

The US funds the war by selling US treasury bonds to China and Japan. To make them more competitive, the Fed agrees to cut interest rates.

Rates go from 6% on the eve of 9/11 to 1.3% in 2003, after the end of the "major combat operations" in Iraq.

This sharp and drastic fall creates the ideal conditions for the subprime mortgage bubble to form.

Banks use falling rates to refinance mortgages at a profit, so they aggressively seek clients regardless of their ability to repay the debt.

The end of major combat boosts insurgency. Jordanian-born Abu Musab al-Zarqawi, who had trained in Afghanistan, leads the jihadist movement.

The "Ramadan Offensive" is launched. The frequency of attacks rises to 50 a day. In the month of November alone, 50 soldiers die and 337 are injured.

Uday and Qusay Hussein, the two sons of Saddam Hussein, are killed after a tipster betrays the location of their hideout in Mosul.

President Bush comments on their deaths, stating, "The former regime is gone and will not be coming back."

In order to convince a disbelieving Iraqi public, the Pentagon releases photos and video of the dead bodies of the two brothers, known for wielding vast power through terror.

The Husseins' deaths don't end the Iraqi resistance, as attacks on coalition forces actually increase.

The Federal Reserve continues to cut interest rates to fund the US war-inflated debt. Mortgage rates in the US plunge to 30-year lows and homeowners rush to refinance their loans.

By the end of 2003, the number of mortgage loans granted in the US nearly quadruples from 2000.

The *New York Times* puts the spotlight on Fannie Mae, the financial institution that processes most US mortgages. It describes it as a much bigger risk than publicly disclosed.

The *Financial Times* calls Fannie Mae and Freddie Mac "the Achilles heels of the US financial system."

Computer models suggest that a 1.5% spike in interest rates would trigger a loss of $7.5bn for Fannie Mae.

Parmalat, the Italian dairy and food company and leading manufacturer of ultra-high temperature milk, goes bust after the discovery of a $14bn hole in its account.

The bankruptcy of Parmalat is the largest ever in Europe. Analysts at Commerzbank describe it as "a bombshell."

It emerges that since the beginning of the 1990s Parmalat had been in deep financial troubles, resorting even to falsifying bank accounts. Parmalat becomes "Europe's Enron."

The Italian government rushes to protect 36,400 employees by approving a new law concerning bankruptcy that enables Parmalat to restructure.

Parmalat sues Bank of America, Citigroup, Deloitte & Touche, and Grant Thornton to seek "recovery from third parties believed to have played a central role in its collapse."

"Bank of America assisted certain Parmalat senior managers in structuring and executing a series of complex, mostly off-balance sheet financial transactions that were deliberately designed to conceal Parmalat's insolvency," reads the Parmalat lawsuit.

Warren Buffett, US billionaire and investor, warns against the growing trade of derivatives that he describes as "an investment time bomb" posing serious systemic risk.

Buffett equates the complexity of newly invented derivative instruments to "financial weapons of mass destruction."

The Recording Industry Association of America begins cracking down on those who have illegally swapped more than 1,000 songs over the Internet. It files lawsuits against hundreds of people, including a 12-year-old girl.

Michael Jackson is booked on suspicion of child molestation after two days of searching his famed Neverland Ranch in Santa Barbara.

AOL Time Warner disbands Netscape Communications Corporation. The Mozilla Foundation is established on the same day.

Apple makes downloading both affordable and easy with its iTunes Music Store, which allows fans to download tunes for 99 cents a song.

With over 200,000 songs when launched, iTunes sells more than 1m downloads in the US in just two weeks; by 2008 the iTunes store would become the top music vendor in America.

MySpace, the social network, is launched. In June 2006 it will become the most popular social networking site in the United States, a position that it will hold until 2008.

Google becomes the most popular search engine with 150m enquires a day, beating its rival Yahoo!.

Bill Gates' Microsoft approaches Google for a possible merger of the two companies, but Google declines and unveils plans for a $15.5bn sale of its shares on the open market.

Google is a profitable company, making around \$155.6m a year, thanks to the sale of sponsored links to advertisers.

Skype, a software application that allows users to make voice calls over the Internet, is launched. By 2010 it will have 663m registered users.

From mid-2001 to mid-2003, more than 500,000 technology jobs are lost in the US.

Andrew S. Grove, Intel's co-founder and chair, warns that US dominance in key technological sectors could end, jeopardizing the country's economic recovery and future growth.

"I'm here to be the skunk at your garden party," Grove says during a global technology summit in Washington. He singles out China and India as the main competitors.

The Gartner Group, a market research firm, estimates that by 2004 10% of jobs in the US information technology sector will move offshore, and by 2010 India will surpass the US in the number of people employed in software and technology.

China becomes the third nation in history to launch a man in space in an independent program after the US and USSR. Its first manned space mission is called Shenzhou 5.

It is "an honor for our great motherland, an indicator for the initial victory of the country's first manned space flight, and a historic step taken by the Chinese people in their endeavor to surmount the peak of the world's science and technology," says President Hu Jintao.

Concorde makes its last ever flight over Bristol, England.

A US businessman is diagnosed with SARS, severe acute respiratory syndrome.

He is traveling from China to Singapore when he experiences pneumonia-like symptoms. The plane lands in Hanoi, where he dies soon after.

Carlo Urbani, the World Health Organization (WHO) doctor that assisted him, warns the organization and the world about the danger of the disease. He dies of SARS as well. The WHO launches a global alert.

SARS infects over 8,000 people, killing 916. Within a matter of weeks SARS spreads from Guangdong, China, to 37 countries.

A severe heat wave across Pakistan and India reaches its peak, as temperatures exceed 122°F in the region.

The UK also experiences a heat wave in which the temperature reaches 101.3°F in Kent. It is the first time the UK has recorded a temperature over 100°F.

In France a 111°F heat wave kills approximately 5,000 people, who perish from dehydration and complications of heat-related illnesses.

French authorities use morgues and even warehouses with refrigeration to store the dead bodies.

As many as 60m Americans and Canadians lose electricity on August 14 in one of the biggest blackouts in US history.

Outages stretch from Ohio through much of Pennsylvania, Vermont, New York, Michigan, and the Canadian province of Ontario.

Investigators later trace the outages to three power line failures in Ohio. Fortunately, mild temperatures and even milder temperaments prevail during most of the two-day blackout.

"The Terminator takes on California," headlines the BBC when Arnold Schwarzenegger is elected as governor of California in a decisive victory.

"I know that together we can make this the greatest state in the greatest country in the world," says Schwarzenegger, pledging to reduce the $38bn budget deficit.

Mikhail Khodorkovsky, president and chief executive of the oil company Yukos, is arrested and jailed in October on charges of fraud and tax evasion.

The *Moscow Times* describes his arrest as a "law enforcement agencies' coup d'etat."

Many consider the charges a retaliation for Khodorkovsky's outspoken opposition to President Vladimir Putin.

"There will be no bargaining over the work of law enforcement agencies," Putin declares. "All should be equal before the law, irrespective of how many billions of dollars a person has in his personal or corporate account."

Silvio Berlusconi, prime minister of Italy, insults German MP Martin Schulz by calling him a "kapo," a Nazi prisoner working as a prison guard, during a session of the European Parliament.

In Tbilisi, Georgia, opponents of President Eduard Shevardnadze seize the parliament building and demand the president's resignation.

Following weeks of mass protests over flawed elections, Shevard-nadze resigns.

Luiz Inacio Lula da Silva becomes Brazil's first working-class president. Lula pledges to increase social services and reduce poverty.

Lula creates Bolsa Família and the Ministry of Social Develop-ment. The Bolsa guarantees families $45 a month per child in exchange for making sure the children go to school and follow a prescribed course of vaccinations.

"Lula is everything to me, he's like a guardian angel," Nair Bar-bosa da Rocha, one of the 44m people reached by the program, tells the BBC.

In Argentina, Néstor Carlos Kirchner becomes president. Kirch-ner quickly gains popular support for standing up to military and police officials and for pressuring corrupt justices to resign.

Kirchner pursues a more independent foreign policy, less aligned with the US.

In Paraguay, Nicanor Duarte Frutos wins the presidential elec-tion. In his campaign, he promises public works and opposes privatization.

Belgium legally recognizes same-sex marriage.

The Human Genome Project is completed with 99% of the human genome sequenced to an accuracy of 99.99%.

The first cloned mammal, Dolly the sheep, dies. "The fact that we were able to produce an animal from the cell of another adult . . . had profound effects on biological research and in medicine," says Prof. Ian Wilmut, who led the team that created Dolly in 1996.

NASA's Wilkinson Microwave Anisotropy Probe (WMAP) completes its cosmic microwave background radiation map of the universe, giving scientists a very accurate age of the universe: 13.7bn years.

A nation in mourning, Sweden rejects the euro in a referendum just a few days after Foreign Minister Anna Lindh is stabbed to death in a department store.

The UN lifts sanctions against Libya after the latter agrees to accept responsibility and recompense the families of victims in the 1988 bombing of Pan Am Flight 103.

A series of suicide bombings takes place in Istanbul; a bomb destroys the Turkish head office of HSBC Bank A.S. and the British consulate.

Hamas stages a suicide attack on a bus in Jerusalem that kills 23 Israelis, seven of them children.

Pakistani President Pervez Musharraf narrowly escapes an assassination attempt.

Blasts linked to al-Qaeda kill not only US and coalition members, but also scores of Muslims. In a series of coordinated attacks, hundreds of people are killed in Riyadh, Saudi Arabia; Casablanca, Morocco; and Jakarta, Indonesia.

A car-bomb attack on UN headquarters in Iraq kills the agency's top envoy, Sergio Vieira de Mello, and 21 other employees.

While the Bush administration claims a major victory with the capture of Khalid Shaikh Mohammed, who masterminded 9/11, critics deride the White House for overlooking the war against al-Qaeda in favor of its effort to topple Saddam Hussein in Iraq.

A UN report warns that a lack of international resolve undermines attempts to curb the flow of money, arms, and supporters to al-Qaeda, which has found "fertile ground" for recruitment efforts in Iraq.

On December 13, the US forces capture Saddam Hussein, who was hidden in a tiny cellar on a farm in Tikrit, his hometown in the northwest of Iraq.

"You will not have to fear the rule of Saddam Hussein ever again. All Iraqis who take the side of freedom have taken the winning side," says Bush to the Iraqi people.

The last episode of the film trilogy *The Lord of the Rings* is released. It becomes the second movie, after *Titanic*, to gross over $1bn worldwide.

The entire trilogy will earn almost $3bn in worldwide box office revenues.

A magnitude 6.6 earthquake devastates the southeast Iranian city of Bam, killing tens of thousands and destroying the citadel of Arg-é Bam.

2004
At a Glance

World GDP: $42.1tn
  US: $11.8tn
  Japan: $4.6tn
  Germany: $2.7tn

World population: 6.391bn

Natural disasters:
- 15 people die in Cuba, Jamaica, and the US state of Florida from Hurricane Charley
- 42 people die in Florida from Hurricane Frances
- 92 people die in Grenada, Florida, Venezuela, and Caribbean islands from Hurricane Ivan
- 3,000 people die and 200,000 are left homeless in Haiti from Hurricane Jeanne
- 100 people die in Japan from Typhoon Tokage
- 40 people die and over 100,000 are left homeless by an earthquake in Japan
- 1 person dies and the town of Hallam, Nebraska, is wiped out by a 2.5-mile-wide tornado
- Dominica is hit by the most destructive earthquake in its history, also felt in Guadeloupe
- An 8.1 magnitude earthquake hits Macquarie Island in the Southern Ocean

US federal debt: $7.379tn
US unemployment: 5.54%

Average oil price: $37.41 per barrel
Annual food price index (2002–2004=100): 112
World military spending: $975bn
  US: $455.3bn
  UK: $47.4bn
  France: $46.2bn
US share of total military spending: 47.8%

Time magazine person of the year: George W. Bush

Nobel Peace Prize winner: Wangari Maathai "for her contribution to sustainable development, democracy, and peace."

Introduction

The Abu Ghraib prison in the outskirts of Baghdad had been used by Saddam Hussein's government to imprison and torture political prisoners. The news that the US military reverted to torture of the current prisoners in this same facility sent shock waves around the world.

Soon investigative journalists find evidence that torture was sanctioned at the top of the US government as "enhanced interrogation methods," and is going on at other US prison facilities around the world, such as the Bagram prison in Afghanistan.

Google launches Gmail and Apple's iTunes sells its two hundred millionth song. Citizen journalism begins to challenge traditional media: news of coalition forces' abuses arrives from Iraq via the Internet. Iraqi blogs unveil the harshness of life in "liberated Iraq."

CBS' *60 Minutes* reveals that US military personnel tortured, raped, and abused Iraqi prisoners inside the infamous Abu Ghraib prison, 20 miles from Baghdad.

Two days later, Seymour M. Hersh writes an article titled "Torture at Abu Ghraib." He reveals that top-ranked US officials knew about what was happening inside Abu Ghraib.

When pictures of Lynndie England, reservist of the US Army, standing alongside naked Iraqi prisoners are leaked to the press, she becomes the symbol of the Abu Ghraib scandal.

In an interview on KCNT-TV, Lynndie confesses to having been "instructed" on how to torture prisoners. She also adds that she wasn't doing "anything out of the ordinary."

The Schlesinger Report, a Pentagon sponsored investigation into the Abu Ghraib scandal, calls the abuses acts of "brutality and purposeless sadism."

The report states that there are "fundamental failures throughout all levels of command, from the soldiers on the ground, to Central Command, and to the Pentagon."

In the aftermath of the Abu Ghraib scandal, journalists begin to investigate US interrogation methods. *Newsweek* reports the usage of a technique among them called water-boarding.

Water-boarding makes victims believe they are drowning. It is universally regarded as a form of torture, including by the US government in past years.

In the aftermath of 9/11, President George W. Bush and Vice President Dick Cheney approve water-boarding as a method of interrogation.

In several European countries, lawsuits are filed against US leaders for war crimes at the International Criminal Court, but none of them are pursued.

The Abu Ghraib scandal marks one of the lowest points for the Bush administration and for the American image abroad.

The CIA practice of kidnapping terrorist suspects and of bringing them to Guantánamo comes into the media spotlight.

"But perhaps no practice so fundamentally challenges the foundations of US and international law as the long-term secret incommunicado detention of al-Qaeda suspects in 'undisclosed locations,'" denounces Human Rights Watch.

"'Disappearances' were a trademark abuse of Latin American military dictatorships in their 'dirty war' on alleged subversion," Human Rights Watch continues. "Now they have become a United States tactic in its conflict with al-Qaeda."

It emerges that torture and abuses are not confined to Abu Ghraib. A Human Rights Watch report on Guantánamo contains testimonies of tortured and abused prisoners.

"All day every day we were stuck in a cage of two meters by two meters. We were allowed out for two minutes a week to have a shower and then returned to the cage," says Asif Iqbal, former inmate at Guantánamo.

About his first few weeks there, he continues, "During the day we were forced to sit in the cell (we couldn't lie down) in total silence. We couldn't lean on the wire fence or stand up and walk around in the cage."

Former Chilean dictator General Augusto Pinochet is put under house arrest after being sued for nine kidnappings and a manslaughter charge.

During the Shia Muslim festival, several bombs go off in Karbala and Baghdad, killing hundreds of people. US authorities claim al-Qaeda is responsible.

A suicide bomber kills Ezzedine Salim, the leader of the Iraqi Interim Governing Council, in Baghdad.

In the city of Falluja, a mob kills four Blackwater mercenaries; their mutilated bodies are paraded inside the city. Videos of this ritual are broadcasted across the world.

Al-Zarqawi, who leads the jihadist insurgency and other groups, takes control of Falluja.

The US assembles 10,000 soldiers to launch an attack against Falluja. Civilians flee the city.

Operation Phantom Fury begins and US military forces describe it as "mopping up."

The *Seattle Times* publishes the first pictures of American soldiers in coffins being transported from Iraq. The army immediately fires the couple who took the photos as the US government's policy is to censor any image of the death toll in Iraq.

The final report of the Iraq Study Group, aimed to find proof of the existence of WMD in Iraq, is released.

"I think it's unlikely that we will find any stockpiles," says Colin Powell a few days before the report's release. David Kay, head of the Iraqi Study Group, resigns before the publication, stating, "I don't think they existed."

The *New York Times* admits that its flawed reporting and lack of skepticism in the build-up to the 2003 war in Iraq helped promote the belief that Iraq possessed large stockpiles of WMD.

Abdul Qadeer Khan, founder of the Pakistani nuclear program, appears on a national television program and admits he had sold nuclear weapons technology to Iran, North Korea, and Libya.

The following day, President Musharraf pardons him. *Time* magazine describes Khan as "the world's most dangerous nuclear trafficker."

The United States lifts the long-standing ban on travels and economic sanctions on Libya as a reward for its cooperation in ending its WMD program.

Mordechai Vanunu, imprisoned in 1986 for revealing that Israel had acquired nuclear weapons, is released. He is not allowed to talk to the international press and cannot leave Israel.

The UN calls for Iran to "immediately" stop enriching uranium. The US lobbies to take decisive action against Iran's secret nuclear program.

Hassan Rohani, principal negotiator of the Iranian nuclear program, declares that if the US and its European allies "sought a complete termination of Iran's nuclear fuel-cycle activities, there would be no space for negotiations."

The 9/11 Commission issues its first report, which states that the threat of al-Qaeda was not understood due to a "failure of imagination."

Michael Moore releases *Fahrenheit 9/11*, a documentary highly critical of Bush, his administration's response to the terrorist attack, and the war in Iraq.

The movie wins the Palm d'Or at the Cannes International Film Festival. *Fahrenheit 9/11* becomes the highest-grossing documentary of all time.

Al Jazeera broadcasts an excerpt from a video of Osama bin Laden in which the terrorist leader admits direct responsibility for the September 11, 2001, attacks.

On March 11, a terrorist attack strikes Madrid's trains while entering Atocha station just three days before the general election in Spain. 191 people die and 1,800 are injured.

To defend his support for the war in Iraq, President Aznar insists that Basque separatist group ETA staged the attack.

Later, the Spanish judiciary finds a jihadist group, inspired by 9/11, to be responsible for the Madrid bombings. Spaniards take to the street to demand clarity and the withdrawal from Iraq.

The Atocha bombing and the Spanish government's handling of it consume the political debate. In the general elections the PSOE, the Socialists Workers Party, defeats Aznar's PP, the People's Party.

With 74% of Spanish electorate against the war in Iraq, Zapatero immediately honors his electoral promise and withdraws the troops from Iraq.

The world economy prospers. The US grows 4.4%, the highest rate in five years. China however continues to outpace everybody else, growing at 9.5%.

The Paris Club, an informal group of official creditors who review debtor countries' positions, agrees to write off 80% (up to $100bn) of Iraq's external debt.

Ronald Reagan dies at his California home, nearly 10 years after announcing that he was suffering from Alzheimer's disease.

The nation spends a week saying farewell to the former president, who led a conservative revolution and helped bring about the end of the Cold War during his two terms in office.

He is laid to rest at the Ronald Reagan Presidential Library in California after a state funeral in Washington DC.

The documentary *Supersize Me* raises concerns about fast food in the US and abroad.

The Atkins diet, high in protein and low in carbs, becomes a great success. The US National Public Radio announces that 1 out of every 11 Americans follows a version of the diet.

New Jersey Governor Jim McGreevy announces that he is having an extramarital affair with another man and is therefore resigning.

Massachusetts becomes the first state in the US to legalize gay marriage.

The city of San Francisco, California, starts to issue marriage licenses to same-sex couples.

69% of Californians vote in favor of a referendum to fund embryonic stem cell research, making the state the first to approve stem cell research.

France passes a law banning head-scarves in schools. The law specifically targets burqa- and niqba-wearing girls.

Prime Minister François Fillon explains the law, saying, "The French Republic lives in a bare-headed fashion." Critics say the ban represents a violation of religious freedom.

The UN International Court of Justice declares illegal the wall between Israel and the occupied territories, ordering Israel to stop its construction. Israel doesn't comply.

Human Rights Watch declares that the wall is a serious violation of human rights and international humanitarian law because it imposes severe restrictions on freedom of movement, causing extensive and disproportionate harm to Palestinians.

An Israeli airstrike kills Abdel Aziz al-Rantissi, one of the leaders of Hamas, while he is riding in his car in Gaza.

Yasser Arafat, head of the Palestine Liberation Organization, dies in Paris. He is the symbol of the Palestinian cause.

In 1994 he shared the Nobel Peace Prize with Yitzhak Rabin and Shimon Peres, the Israeli prime minister and foreign minister, for their efforts to promote peace between Palestine and Israel. However, Arafat was also seen by some as a terrorist.

While many mourn his passing, others see his death as an opportunity for Palestinians and Israelis to reinvigorate the peace talks.

The Sudanese government and two rebel groups sign a ceasefire agreement, ending the country's 21-year civil war.

Poland, Lithuania, Latvia, Estonia, the Czech Republic, Slovakia, Slovenia, Hungary, Malta, and Cyprus become part of the EU.

The first European Constitution is born, boosting cohesion within the EU.

Representatives from 12 South American nations sign the Cusco declaration, the embryo of the Union of South American Nations (UNASUR), inspired by the EU.

Cuba and Venezuela sign the Peoples' Trade Agreement, the first step of the Bolivarian Alliance for the Americas (ALBA).

Russia ratifies the Kyoto Protocol, which enters into force the following year. The United States, the second biggest polluter, refuses to ratify it.

Bulgaria, Estonia, Latvia, Lithuania, Romania, Slovakia, and Slovenia join NATO as full members. Russia condemns the expansion.

Riots targeting the Serbian population in Kosovo drive thousands of Serbs from their homes.

The riots start after a false rumor about a Serbian man drowning two Kosovo Albanian children spreads.

A bomb placed under the VIP section of the Dinamo football stadium in Grozny explodes, killing Chechen president Akhmad Kadyrov and several other people.

Chechen terrorists take hostage 1,138 children in a school in Beslan, Russia. When the police break into the building, 331 people die in the shooting.

Viktor Yanukovych wins the Ukrainian presidential election during a campaign marked by biased media and accusations of electoral fraud.

The election reflects a clash between East and West, rural versus urban culture. Russia backs Yanukovych, who is strong in the rural areas, while the Western-friendly Yushchenko draws support from cities.

Following the election, thousands of people take to the streets every day to protest the outcome of the election in what becomes known as the Orange Revolution.

The Supreme Court rules that a new election needs to be held. Yushchenko wins 52% of the vote and is declared the official winner.

Current Interim President Hamid Karzai wins the election in Afghanistan despite serious accusations of electoral fraud.

Left-wing candidate Tabaré Vázquez is elected president of Uruguay. He campaigns on a platform of social justice.

Before the Republican Party convention, 200,000 people gather to protest against President George W. Bush in New York.

Nationwide, voters turn out in droves, with a turnout rate approaching 60%, the highest since 1968.

Exit polls suggest voters who cited "moral values" as the most important element in making their decision may have assured President Bush a second term.

In the 11 gubernatorial races, Democrats and Republicans split 10 contests while Washington's race remains too close to call and the state undertakes a hand recount.

As in 2000, the presidential election comes down to one state. This time, it is Ohio's 20 electoral votes that put Bush over the top. Unlike 2000, Bush also wins the popular vote, with 51% to Kerry's 48%.

The election further tips the balance of power decisively into the Republican sphere as the party wins larger advantages in both the Senate and the House.

An al-Qaeda commando attacks the US consulate in Jeddah, Saudi Arabia, killing several people.

Oil prices surge over $40 a barrel upon fear of an interruption of supply from Saudi Arabia. EU countries call an emergency meeting to deal with "record-high oil prices."

The EU fines Bill Gates' Microsoft €497m for abusing its dominant role in the market of personal computer software. The fine is the largest ever imposed by EU authorities.

The US authorities also impose a fine on Microsoft. However, many describe the fines as "traffic tickets" compared to the $53bn cash profits of the company.

Chinese PC maker Lenovo announces its plan to buy IBM's global PC business, making it the third largest PC company in the world after Dell and Hewlett-Packard.

While the Internet makes the world more interconnected, North Korea bans mobile phones.

Google issues shares to the public for the first time. The total value of the shares at its initial public offering is "only" $24bn. However, by the end of the year the price of its shares almost quadruples.

Google launches Gmail.

Apple's iTunes sells its 200,000,000th song. According to Nielsen SoundScan, music fans bought 5.5m digital albums and 140m digital songs.

The final episode of *Friends* goes on air. The sitcom has run for 10 consecutive years. 52.5m Americans watch the final episode, making it the most popular show of the decade.

Mel Gibson's *The Passion of the Christ* grosses $89.3m in its first three days in theaters. It becomes the third–highest grossing film of the year, taking in $370m.

The film, in Latin and Aramaic with English subtitles, depicts the last 12 hours of Jesus's life in explicitly violent detail.

Many deride the film as anti-Semitic, saying it casts blame on the Jews for Jesus Christ's crucifixion.

A number of evangelical Christian and Catholic groups, however, praise the film for its portrayal of Jesus Christ's sacrifice.

Over 600 Muslims are killed by Christians in the Yelwa massacre in Nigeria.

One of the world's poorest nations, Bangladesh suffers yet another flood. Water covers 60% of the nation. The UN estimates that the floods affect 30m people.

On the day after Christmas, seismographs record the third largest earthquake ever at the bottom of the Indian Ocean.

The tsunami generated hits Southeast Asia, killing over 200,000 people from Thailand to Somalia. Waves reach a height of 20 to 30 feet.

The tsunami leaves hundreds of thousands without homes, food, fresh water, or power, and strikes both impoverished villages and rich tourist sites, sparing few areas in its path.

The United Nations urges donor countries to contribute materials and money, saying this could be the costliest disaster ever. $127m is donated.

The aid raised amounts to an estimated $7,100 per victim, as compared to the flood victims in Bangladesh the same year, who received only $3 per victim.

The tsunami comes several weeks after the close of one of the most active Atlantic hurricane seasons in recent years.

By late summer, several major storms hit Florida, the US East Coast, and the Caribbean.

2005
At a Glance

World GDP: $45.6tn
  US: $12.5tn
  Japan: $4.5tn
  Germany: $2.7tn

World population: 6.467bn

Natural disasters:
  75,000 people die in an earthquake in the Kashmir region in Pakistan
  Over 500 people die in two earthquakes in Iran
  22 named storms, including Hurricane Katrina, form in the Atlantic Basin, the most active Atlantic hurricane season on record
  Over 1,000 people die in Central America from Hurricane Stan
  10 people die, Highway 101 is closed for 10 days by a mudslide in California
  1 person dies, hundreds are injured in an earthquake in Japan
  Billions of dollars in damage to the Florida Panhandle are caused by Hurricane Dennis
  2 people die and nearly 100 homes are destroyed in Wright, Wyoming, by a tornado
  25 die in Kentucky and Indiana from the Evansville Tornado

US federal debt: $7.932tn
US unemployment: 5.08%

Average oil price: $50.04 per barrel

Annual food price index (2002–2004=100): 117.3
World military spending: $1.001tn
  US: $478.2bn
  UK: $48.3bn
  France: $46.2bn
US share of total military spending: 47.8%

Time magazine people of the year: The Good Samaritans, Bill Gates, Melinda Gates, and Bono of the pop group U2

Nobel Peace Prize winner: International Atomic Energy Agency and Mohamed ElBaradei "for their efforts to prevent nuclear energy from being used for military purposes and to ensure that nuclear energy for peaceful purposes is used in the safest possible way."

Introduction

Hurricane Katrina exposes the weakness of the US to the world, a shocking discovery. President Bush's approval ratings plummet to 40% after the poor handling of the tragedy, then an all-time low.

   A few former employees of PayPal launch YouTube to share videos among friends. Communication will never be the same, nor will political protest, as YouTube will empower people beyond anybody's imagination.

On August 29, 2005, Hurricane Katrina hits New Orleans. After poorly maintained levees collapse, water floods 80% of New Orleans.

The National Hurricane Center alerts the public, and the Bush administration advises the population to flee New Orleans.

Poor evacuation plans coupled with thousands of people who cannot afford to flee the city provoke a very high death toll.

When Katrina strikes, 40% of the Louisiana National Guard is in Iraq. With most of the country's reserves abroad, it takes days to rescue people.

Katrina becomes one of the five deadliest hurricanes ever to strike the US, killing over 1,700 people.

The media defines the damage inflicted on Louisiana and Mississippi as "staggering."

"New Orleans may never be the same," says Max Mayfield, director of the National Hurricane Center.

More than 40 corpses of patients are discovered in a flooded hospital in New Orleans.

Bush doesn't cut short his vacation, eventually returning to Washington two days after the hurricane. Thousands of Americans, including actor Sean Penn, rush to New Orleans to participate in rescue operations.

In the aftermath, the media reports stories of looting, hijacking, and rape. However, news desks are later forced to admit that much of this news was false.

Katrina shows the world an unknown face of America: racially divided and inefficient, the portrait of a superpower with third world social and economic traits.

"I hate the way they portray us in the media," says rapper Kanye West. "If you see a black family, it says they are looting; if you see a white family, it says that they are looking for food."

In a moment that would spread virally on YouTube and other social media networks, West proclaims in a live broadcast, "George Bush doesn't care about black people."

Criticism about the handling of the crisis mounts. Governor of Louisiana Kathleen Blanco and President Bush claim that nobody has fully briefed them about the risk of the floods.

Though the US government waits almost a week before requesting international assistance, the response is quick.

Venezuela offers food, water, and millions of barrels of fuel. Other countries that have frosty relationships with the US also offer help, among them Cuba, Iran, and China.

Americans donate $514m in just one week to US public authorities and NGOs to help the victims.

During the first month, FEMA grants contracts for $11.6bn for cleaning and rebuilding.

Resources aren't sufficient and corruption becomes rampant. Senior officials from the Department of Homeland Security confess to be "very apprehensive" about the process of contract awarding.

Halliburton, formerly headed by Vice President Dick Cheney, secures a large chunk of the contracts. In a month, its shares are up 20%.

Thomas Friedman publishes *The World Is Flat*. He believes that modern, technology-driven globalization is leveling the playing field for economic opportunities across the world.

The debt-to-finance consumption ratio rises exponentially in Western markets. US household debt reaches almost 140% of GDP. Savings shrink to 1% from 10% in 1970.

Raghuram Rajan, chief economist of the International Monetary Fund, delivers a paper at the Jackson Hole symposium where central bankers from all over the world meet yearly.

The paper is entitled "Has financial development made the world riskier?" Raghuram Rajan concludes that it has.

The chief economist of the IMF criticizes cash incentives to investment bankers, the bonus schemes that reward short-term profit and punish long-term losses.

These incentives push bankers to take excessive risks that might result in a "full-blown financial crisis," he says. Central bankers and regulators in New York and London dismiss the warning.

In the UK, the Labour Party wins the general elections and Tony Blair remains prime minister. But he promises to hand over the leadership to Gordon Brown before the term ends.

On July 7, London suffers four simultaneous terrorist attacks: three in the subway and one on a bus. 56 people die and nearly 1,000 are injured.

Prime Minister Tony Blair says that "evil ideology" had motivated the London bombers.

64% of Britons blame the London bombings on Prime Minister Tony Blair's decision to go to war in Iraq. The *Guardian* argues that it was "common sense" to assume that the war would increase the risk of terrorist attacks.

In a video, one of the suicide bombers blames the attack on the humiliation of Muslims in occupied Iraq.

Research published by Technorati, an Internet company, claims that a new blog is born every second. Japan, Korea, China, France, and Brazil are regarded as areas of high growth.

Leslie Bunder, editor of the technology blog Journalistic.co.uk, says terrorism draws people to start their own blogs, thus creating citizen journalism.

"July 7 in London gave rise to people realizing they could do the news themselves," he says. "There [were] a lot of blogs feeding the news media with stories and information."

A few former employees of PayPal start YouTube, a popular Internet site where videos may be shared and viewed by others.

They create YouTube because they had difficulties sharing on the web a video they shot at a party.

The first video posted on YouTube shows founder Jawed Karim at the San Diego Zoo, and it is entitled "Me at the zoo."

Within a year YouTube reaches an enormous audience, becoming the symbol of a generation and inspiring *Time*'s person of the year of 2006.

People registered in the social network MySpace become the first users and unintended promoters of YouTube.

Rupert Murdoch, the Australian owner of Fox News and 20th Century Fox, buys MySpace for $580m.

Murdoch launches MySpace Records to discover new music talents using the social networking website.

Lily Allen begins her music career posting demos on MySpace. Thousands listen to her in a matter of weeks.

Five suicide bombers fail to detonate themselves in London's Tube.

The following day, the police chase Jean Charles de Menezes, a Brazilian electrician they mistake for a jihadist, and kill him at point-blank range with seven bullets to the head in front of horrified commuters.

Suicide bombers attack three hotels in Amman, Jordan, killing at least 60 people. They are linked to al-Zarqawi.

Iraqis hold their first democratic elections. Major parties boycott them because coalition forces have organized the election.

Iraqis see the election as a way for the coalition to pretend that Iraq isn't occupied by foreign troops.

In Baghdad, tens of thousands of people demanding the withdrawal of coalition forces mark the anniversary of the fall of Saddam Hussein's regime.

The protesters gather in Firdos Square, in central Baghdad, where American troops and Iraqis pulled down the huge statue of Hussein in 2003.

The Democratic Patriotic Alliance of Kurdistan, a Kurdish list that represents the Kurdish minority in Northen Iraq, becomes the second largest party with 26% of the vote.

It is revealed that the US military has placed articles in Iraqi newspapers under the guise of independent journalism.

A suicide bomb explodes in a police recruitment center in Iraq, killing at least 60 people. The attack is just one of many against people willing to work with coalition forces.

Italian journalist Giuliana Sgrena is kidnapped in Iraq. After a few weeks the Italian secret service rescues her and takes her to the airport.

American soldiers at a checkpoint open fire on the car where Sgrena is travelling. Nicola Calipari, head of the Italian secret agency in Iraq, dies along with another agent.

Sgrena describes the incident as "an execution." She is well known for her opposition to the war and for her sympathy for the Iraqi people.

The shooting spurs a diplomatic incident between the US and Italy, prompting several parallel investigations into what happened, with completely different conclusions.

A military jury convicts Lynndie England for the Abu Ghraib torture scandal.

Officials argue that England and her friends initiated the torture and the abuses. However, several sources claim it was a standard operating procedure encouraged by commanders.

Saddam Hussein goes on trial in Baghdad for crimes against humanity.

North Korea announces that it has acquired nuclear weapons. "In response to the Bush administration's increasingly hostile policy toward North Korea, we . . . have manufactured nuclear weapons for self-defense."

North Korea accuses Bush of intentionally attempting to "antagonize, isolate, and stifle [North Korea] at any cost." Newly appointed Secretary of State Condoleezza Rice calls North Korea an "outpost of tyranny."

On the eve of a meeting of Non-Proliferation Treaty members, Pyongyang shoots a short-range missile in the Sea of Japan.

In Iran, hardline conservative Mahmoud Ahmadinejad wins the general election in a landslide victory.

In his campaign Ahmadinejad promises to turn Iran into a main regional power, in part by developing nuclear capabilities.

North Korea agrees to abandon its nuclear weapons program in exchange for a nuclear civil reactor. Rice responds coldly, "The prospect is some time in the future."

David Asher, a Bush administration adviser on North Korea, calls it "a criminal state," accusing Pyongyang of financing its nuclear program with illicit activities such as narco-trafficking.

"This is state-sponsored counterfeiting. I don't know of any other case like this except the Nazis, and they were doing it in a state of war," says Asher.

According to the Organisation for Economic Co-operation and Development (OECD), the value of international trade in counterfeit and pirated products is $200bn, not including domestic and digital trade.

Besides clothes and DVDs, counterfeit goods include pharmaceutical products, medical equipment, tobacco, and automotive parts.

The first direct commercial flights from mainland China to Taiwan since 1949 arrive in Taipei.

The aircraft Airbus A380 makes its first flight from Toulouse, France.

The first partial human face transplant is completed in Amiens, France.

The TV show *The Osbournes* airs for the last time. The family life and everyday challenges of heavy-metal singer Ozzy Osbourne had become the most watched series ever on MTV.

A series of concerts called Live 8, a call to action to end poverty in third world countries, precede the G8 meeting in Scotland.

Influenced by Live 8, the G8 leaders pledge to double 2004 levels of aid to Africa from $25bn to $50bn by the year 2010. These promises are never honored.

The United Nations warns that about 90m Africans can be infected by HIV in the future if no action is taken against the spread of the disease.

The WHO argues that 2m people die prematurely because of air pollution. Half of them reside in developing countries.

The Kyoto Protocol goes into effect, without the support of the US and Australia.

Same-sex marriage becomes legal in Canada, Spain, and the UK, while in Latvia the constitution is amended to eliminate the possibility of same-sex marriages.

Spain offers amnesty to nearly 800,000 illegal immigrants working in the country.

Socialist candidate Evo Morales becomes president of Bolivia. He is the first Bolivian president of indigenous descent.

A jury in Santa Maria, California, frees pop singer Michael Jackson from charges of molesting 13-year-old Gavin Arvizo at his Neverland Ranch.

Israel officially hands over Jericho to Palestinian control.

Israel evicts all Jewish citizens from the Gaza strip and from four settlements on the West Bank.

Following the assassination of Lebanon's former prime minister Rafik Hariri, the country falls into turmoil. Amid large anti-Syrian street demonstrations in Beirut, Lebanon's pro-Syrian prime minister Omar Karami resigns.

Over 1.5m Lebanese people pour into the streets of Beirut to demonstrate against Syrian military presence in the country; the protests are dubbed the Cedar Revolution.

Facing mounting international pressure, Syria withdraws its last military troops from Lebanon. This ends Syria's 30-year military presence in the country.

In Yemen, the US rewards the government's counterterrorism unit with equipment and weapons after the arrest of al-Qaeda–linked terrorists.

The income gap between rich and poor in Yemen keeps growing, while politics become more polarized between the ruling party and the opposition in the country. The stage is being set for the 2011 uprisings.

Three bombs explode in the Naama Bay area of Sharm el-Sheikh, Egypt, killing 88 people.

The Danish newspaper *Jyllands-Posten* publishes degrading drawings of the prophet Muhammad to provoke Muslims.

The drawings trigger protests throughout the Muslim world and a boycott of Danish merchandise.

In Paris, riots erupt in the poorest neighborhoods surrounding the city after police cause the deaths of two Muslim teenagers.

In a referendum, the French and the Dutch reject the European Constitution.

After the elections, negotiations between three German political parties lead to the formation of a grand coalition under the leadership of Angela Merkel. She is Germany's first female chancellor.

Millions of people mourn the death of Pope John Paul II. On the second day of the papal conclave, Cardinal Joseph Ratzinger becomes Pope Benedict XVI.

Benedict XVI is the 265th pope of the Roman Catholic Church.

A Chinese company, Cnooc, bids to buy the American oil company Unocal. The Chinese withdraw their bid after it raises a political firestorm in Washington over economic security and economic competition with China.

Laptops outsell desktops over a month-long period for the first time, making it a milestone in PC sales history.

Microsoft releases its new video game console, Xbox 360, which is the most powerful consol on the market.

Sudoku gains worldwide popularity. Soon nearly every newspaper includes Sudoku puzzles.

Sales of flat-screen TVs skyrocket after prices drop. "Slim-TV sales anything but flat," reads a CNET headline.

Google launches Google Earth, a virtual globe map and geographical information program that maps the earth from images obtained by satellites.

Mumbai, India, receives 39 inches of rain within 24 hours, bringing the city to a halt for over two days.

An earthquake hits Pakistan, Afghanistan, and India, leaving about 75,000 people dead and hundreds of thousands homeless.

2006
At a Glance

World GDP: $49.4tn
  US: $13.3tn
  Japan: $4.3tn
  Germany: $2.9tn

World population: 6.543bn

Natural disasters:
  6,000 people die and over 1m people become homeless in an
    earthquake in Java
  Over 1,000 people die in Typhoon Durian in the Philippines
  An earthquake hits much of Greece and is felt throughout the
    entire eastern Mediterranean Sea
  Cyclone Larry creates a landfall in eastern Australia, destroying
    most of the country's banana crop.
  Over 60 tornadoes break out in the US, 29 people die in Ten-
    nessee
  A large earthquake occurs near New Zealand
  The Hengchun earthquake hits Taiwan

US federal debt: $8.506tn
US unemployment: 4.6%

Average oil price: $58.30 per barrel
Annual food price index (2002–2004=100): 126.5

World military spending: $1.158tn
  US: $528.7bn

UK: $59bn
France: $53.1bn
US share of total military spending: 45.7%

Time magazine person of the year: You

Nobel Peace Prize winners: Muhammad Yunus and Grameen Bank "for their efforts to create economic and social development from below."

Introduction

In 2006, the Middle East is on fire. Hamas wins the Palestinian election. War breaks out in Lebanon. Iraq slides into civil war and tension with Iran escalates.

But 2006 is also the year of digital success. WikiLeaks is launched, Silicon Valley explores the potential of Web 2.0, 65,000 videos are uploaded on YouTube every day, MySpace announces its one hundred millionth account, and Facebook redesigns people's social relations. Finally, Wikipedia takes off with people contributing on a daily basis to the annals of their own history.

Israeli Prime Minister Ariel Sharon suffers a massive stroke, ending his political career. Ehud Olmert steps in as acting prime minister.

After much encouragement by US Secretary of State Condoleezza Rice, the Palestinian people hold their first elections for Legislative Council since 1996. The Islamist group Hamas wins a landslide victory, securing 74 seats in the 132-seat council.

People refuse to vote for Western-backed Fatah, the other major party, because of accusations of corruption and bribery.

The Israeli government declares that it will not negotiate with any Palestinian government that includes members of Hamas.

US President George W. Bush echoes the Israeli sentiment and states that the US will not deal with Hamas unless it renounces its call to destroy Israel.

Hamas leader Ismail Haniya responds that as long as "the Israelis continue their aggression against our people we will defend ourselves using all means, including guns."

"Today Hamastan was formed, a representative of Iran and in the image of the Taliban," says

Benjamin Netanyahu, leader of Israeli opposition party Likud at the time.

Following the victory of Hamas, Israel imposes economic sanctions on the Palestinian territories. Western leaders announce they will boycott Hamas and back appointed president Mahmoud Abbas, leader of Fatah.

Frustrated by the situation, Amr Moussa, Arab League Secretary General, declares, "[T]he US can't promote democracy and then reject its electoral outcome."

Sydney, Australia, swelters through its hottest New Year's Day on record. The thermometer peaks at 113°F, sparking bushfires and power outages.

Saddam Hussein testifies for the first time in his trial where he faces charges for genocide and crimes against humanity for the gassing of Kurds in 1988 and the killing of 148 Shiite boys in 1982.

The trial ends after nine months. Saddam is sentenced to death by hanging, and on December 30, the sentence is carried out.

Someone films his hanging on a cell phone and the video spreads online and in TV news; the world watches Saddam die.

The *New York Times* writes that the National Intelligence Council believes the Iraq war breeds a deep resentment toward the US involvement in the Muslim world and helps recruit people for the jihadist movement.

The chief of the British Army, General Richard Dannatt, tells newspapers that Britain's presence in Iraq has made the country less secure.

Reconstruction projects in Iraq are still delayed; waste and corruption are rampant. Special Inspector General Stuart Bowen Jr., investigates 72 firms involved in reconstruction for corruption.

The Government Accountability Office (GAO), an independent branch of the US Congress, describes the Bush administration's strategy in Iraq as "inadequate and poorly planned."

GAO also reports that the administration does not demand accountability for the $1.5bn per week that the United States spends in Iraq.

After government audits discover $1bn in unaccounted and questionable costs, the US government ends its multi-billion dollar contract with Halliburton to provide logistical support in Iraq.

The US military and Iraqi forces launch "Operation Swarmer," a massive attack against insurgents and the largest air assault since the beginning of the war.

Insurgent leader (and head of al-Qaeda in Iraq) al-Zarqawi dies in a US airstrike. Muqtada al-Sadr emerges as a religious leader of the Shia Muslims.

At the end of the year al-Sadr goes into exile to Iran, vowing not to return until the occupiers leave Iraq. But he will come back one year later.

WikiLeaks' website is launched. Its aim is to shed light on government misuse of power. Its mysterious spokesperson, Julian Assange, will become well known in the coming years.

In 2006, the idea of a Web 2.0, based on user interaction and participation, gains traction as Silicon Valley consultants begin realizing the potential of the new World Wide Web.

YouTube announces that 65,000 videos are uploaded every day and that there are 100m viewers per day.

MySpace announces its 100,000,000th account. MySpace has become the most popular social networking site.

In 2006, over 1,800 articles are added each day on Wikipedia. English-language Wikipedia reaches its 1,000,000th article: "Jordanhill railway station."

Talking about the Abu Ghraib prison scandal, Bush admits that it is "the biggest mistake that's happened so far, at least from our country's involvement in Iraq. We've been paying for that for a long period of time."

Blair acknowledges that it is too early to plan a pullout from Iraq. "Inevitably, over time, we have to transfer responsibility. But as for now," he says, "the Iraqi government has said they want us to stay until the job is done."

The foreign ministers of the UK, France, and Germany declare that negotiations with Iran over its nuclear program have reached a dead end and recommend that the UN Security Council deal with Iran's nuclear program.

Iranian President Mahmoud Ahmadinejad announces that Iran has successfully enriched uranium.

A Holocaust review conference takes place in Tehran, Iran. The presence of Holocaust deniers stirs criticism.

North Korea tests four short-range missiles. One of them fails in mid-air over the Sea of Japan. More missiles are launched, prompting an emergency UN Security Council meeting.

Later in the year, North Korea tests its first nuclear device.

Human Rights Watch denounces extraordinary rendition, the abduction of people suspected to be terrorists to be handed over to ally countries, where they are often tortured.

On a visit to Egypt, FBI Director Robert Mueller agrees to keep Egyptian authorities informed of the Muslim Brotherhood's activities in the US.

Despite the dictatorship's infamous reputation of torturing and harassing prisoners, Mueller proposes to share technology and information with the Egyptian security service.

In 2010, WikiLeaks will reveal that the Egyptian security service received training at the FBI academy in Quantico, Virginia, and that the two countries shared fingerprint files.

According to the head of the Egyptian secret service, Abdul Rahman, the relationship between the two agencies was "solid" and "strong."

In the *Hamdan v. Rumsfeld* case, the US Supreme Court rules that President George W. Bush's plan to try Guantánamo Bay detainees in military tribunals violates US and international law.

Hezbollah, a Lebanese militant group, fires rockets into Israel. Israel bombs Beirut International Airport in retaliation.

The war between Israel and Lebanon lasts 34 days, killing 1,200 people. Lebanon suffers the most, with large sections of the south uninhabitable due to unexploded Israeli bombs.

Human Rights Watch publishes a report accusing Israel of "indiscriminate attacks against civilians in Lebanon." Amnesty International reports Hezbollah violated humanitarian law by firing more than 4,000 rockets onto civilians during the war.

Israel imposes an air and sea blockade on Lebanon, which affects the population. The blockade is lifted in September after both parties adhere to a UN resolution calling for hostilities to stop.

Late in the year, 1m Lebanese gather in downtown Beirut, calling for the government to resign.

British police stop a terrorist plot to detonate liquid explosives aboard several airplanes crossing the Atlantic. Containers of liquid larger than 3 oz are banned from planes.

Years later, British courts will rule that the so-called liquid bomb never existed, but airports continue to ban liquids on flights.

Dubai Ports World agrees to postpone its plans to take over the management of six US ports after the proposal ignites harsh criticism in Washington.

ETA, the armed Basque separatist group, declares a permanent ceasefire.

Thousands of public sector workers and students go on strike and protest against changes in labor regulations in Great Britain and France.

The proposed changes make it easier for employers to fire workers under the age of 26. After the protests, French president Jacques Chirac repeals the law.

The Republic of Montenegro holds a referendum proposing independence from the State Union of Serbia and Montenegro. The Montenegrin people choose independence with a majority of 55%.

Guinea Bissau seizes 600 kg of cocaine destined for Europe; its street value amounts to 1/3 of Guinea Bissau's GDP.

West Africa has become the key hub for drugs and other illicit trades from Latin America to the growing market of Europe.

The number of European consumers of illicit drugs has risen, with Spain, the UK, and Italy as top consumers of cocaine imported from Latin America.

Colombia produces the vast majority of the cocaine consumed in the world. Mexico, on the other hand, is at the forefront of the production and distribution of marijuana, a business that generates $8.6bn annually.

Newly elected president Felipe Calderon declares war against illicit drugs in Mexico. His strategy involves the use of force, with the help of the military, against drug traffickers.

At the beginning of 2006, Russia and Ukraine dispute the price of natural gas. Russia, which subsidizes natural gas for the former Soviet Block countries in return for political support, ends the subsidy to the pro-Western government in Ukraine.

Gazprom, the Russian oil and gas giant that supplies a quarter of Europe's gas mainly via Kiev, wants to renew the deal at double the price.

When the price increase is rejected, Gazprom halts gas supplies in the middle of winter. Russia also accuses Ukraine of stealing $25m of gas exports destined to Europe.

The movie *An Inconvenient Truth* premiers at the Sundance Film Festival, as well as at theaters in New York and Los Angeles.

The movie raises awareness about the environment and calls for action to do something about it. It prompts climate issues to be placed at the top of the political agenda in many countries.

A landslide in the Philippines buries a village and over a thousand people.

Harnessing the power of Web 2.0, Google purchases YouTube for $1.65bn.

The BBC also embraces Web 2.0 and announces major changes in its Internet content. The philosophy of sharing will be at the heart of the bbc.co.uk 2.0 website.

BBC's technology director Ashley Highfield calls the project a "radical plan to rebuild its website around user-generated content, including blogs and home-videos."

The US social networking website Facebook, once open only to students and workplace networks, widens its spectrum of users by allowing anybody above the age of 13 to access its services.

Facebook also announces the introduction of a news feed, which highlights any changes in friends' profiles or statuses instantly.

Facebook's strategic moves takes the website from being the 60th in worldwide Internet traffic to becoming the 7th in one year.

The biannual research study conducted by Student Monitor in US colleges lists the three most popular items: Apple's iPods came in first, beer second, and Facebook third.

China clamps down on Internet freedom and effectively imposes restrictions on Google, Microsoft, Baidu, and Yahoo!. Officials list 19 websites that harm young people's physical and mental health.

Internet freedom is also threatened elsewhere. In 2006, the EU issues the data retention directive, enabling law enforcement agencies to, for example, access individuals' e-mails, phone calls, and text messages.

The pope infuriates the Muslim world by quoting old scripts, saying, "Show me just what Mohammed brought that was new, and there you will find things only evil and inhuman, such as his command to spread by the sword the faith he preached."

For Muslim Brotherhood Chairman Mohammed Mahdi Akef, "the pope's statement came to add fuel to fire and trigger anger within the Muslim world and show that the West with its politicians and clerics are hostile to Islam."

Italy wins the soccer World Cup in Germany, defeating France on penalties. France's star player Zinedine Zidane is sent off toward the end of the game for head-butting Italy's Marco Materazzi.

The World Cup is broadcasted in HD-format, now the most widely used by consumers.

Sony releases the PlayStation 3, the first video game console to support high definition technology, improving graphics.

Nintendo releases its video game console Wii. Nintendo Wii senses physical gestures, allowing for games to be controlled by the player's movements.

Wi-Fi technology is becoming increasingly available in cafes around the world.

Founded in 2003, Internet networking site LinkedIn becomes profitable in 2006.

Socialist Michelle Bachelet wins the second round of the Chilean presidential election, becoming the nation's first female president. She announces that everyone should benefit from the country's growth.

President Bush uses his veto for the first time in order to block a legislation that would lift funding restrictions on human embryonic stem cell research.

In rejecting the bill, Bush says, "It crosses a moral boundary that our decent society needs to respect."

One of the proponents of the bill rejects Bush's claim of a moral boundary, saying, "Those families who wake up every morning to face another day with a deadly disease or a disability will not forget this decision by the president to stand in the way of sound science and medical research."

The US Democratic party wins a landslide victory in the mid-term elections of 2006. Nancy Pelosi becomes the first female Speaker of the House of Representatives.

Across the US and the Western world, the US policy toward Iraq is regarded as the main reason for these election results.

In Germany, Jürgen Tritten, deputy head of the parliamentary Green Party, says, "This was the bill to the White House for their disaster in Iraq."

In the UK, John McDonnell, a ruling Labour Party MP, says, "The message of the American people is clear: there needs to be a major change of direction in Iraq. Just as in Britain, people in the US feel that they have been ill-advised, misled, and ignored."

The Socialist Group in the European Parliament, the body's second-largest group, hails the results as "the beginning of the end of a six-year nightmare for the world."

Al Jazeera launches an English-language channel. Al Jazeera is regarded to be a counterweight to the Western domination of international news media.

Russian journalist Anna Politkovskaya is shot dead in the elevator of her apartment building. She was known for her investigative reports from Chechnya that contradicted official news stories.

Allegations that her death was orchestrated by people within the Russian secret service soon surface, but cannot be proven.

In November, a former Russian secret service agent who defected to the UK, Alexander Litvinenko, dies from radiation poisoning.

Litvinenko has unveiled the workings of the secret service in staging terrorist acts in order to bring Putin to power. He also accused Putin of ordering the murder of Anna Politkovskaya.

In finding Litvinenko's murderer, the trace soon leads to Russia and the secret police. Russian authorities refuse to extradite the suspect to the United Kingdom.

The incident cools down UK-Russian relations.

On December 10, 2006, former Chilean dictator Augusto Pinochet dies. He came to power after a US-backed coup against then-President Salvador Allende in 1973.

Over 200 people die in the bombing of a train in Bombay.

Civilian deaths in Iraq rise. The UN reports that more than 34,000 people have been killed. Iraq Body Count estimates that over 27,000 civilians have died, compared to 15,000 in 2005.

In 2010, WikiLeaks reveals that SIGACTs, US military secret reports, put the number of deaths in Iraq at 109,000, of which 60% are civilians, 20% "enemies," 13% Iraqi security forces, and 4% coalition forces.

According to a US Senate report, insurgent attacks in Iraq have increased by 200% on a year-to-year basis.

In early 2006, Alan Greenspan, head of the Federal Reserve, ends his 20 years of chairmanship.

In 1987, Ronald Reagan had appointed Greenspan; later on George H. W. Bush, Bill Clinton, and George W. Bush confirmed him. President Bush appoints Ben Bernanke chairman of the Fed.

In 2006, the subprime share of US mortgages peaks; since 2003 it has increased almost 300%.

The resale of loans in the US also grows, rising from 5% of the mortgage market in the late 1990s to over 20% in 2006.

Risk managers in top investment banks warn their bosses of the risks caused by subprime lending and excessive securitization.

Jeffrey Kronthal, a bond manager at Merrill Lynch, imposes informal limits on the quantity of specific financial instruments its company can be exposed to.

Merrill Lynch dismisses him and two other bond managers. A similar situation happens at Lehman Brothers.

House prices peak and start to fall in the US.

Nouriel Roubini, professor of economics at New York University, warns about the upcoming crisis. His warnings are ignored, only to be rediscovered after the crisis hits.

He writes several papers and articles, stating, "This is the biggest housing slump in the last four or five decades: every housing indicator is in free fall."

Roubini believes that the US is headed for a recession that will be "much nastier, deeper, and more protracted" than the economic downturn of 2001.

"As the housing sector slumps, the job and income and wage losses in housing will percolate throughout the economy," Roubini says.

John Church and Neil White of the Australian governmental science organization CSIRO publish data that confirm sea-level rise is quickening.

Their model suggests sea-level rise will push typical beach shorelines back by close to 1,000 feet.

The Qinghai-Tibet Railway in China opens. The railway achieves the longtime goal of laying rail on the Tibetan permafrost.

The United States population reaches 300m.

YouTube, MySpace, and Wikipedia inspire *Time* magazine to give the 2006 Person of the Year award to "You." In a stunning front cover, a silver gloss mirror is printed so any reader can see himself or herself reflected.

Time magazine editor Lev Grossman explains why they awarded "You": "for seizing the reins of the global media, for founding and framing the new digital democracy, for working for nothing and beating the pros at their own game."

"Look at 2006 through a different lens and you'll see another story, one that isn't about conflict or great men," he continues. "It's a story about community and collaboration on a scale never seen before."

"It's about the cosmic compendium of knowledge Wikipedia and the million-channel people's network YouTube and the online metropolis MySpace," Lev Grossman writes, focusing on the coming-of-age of Web 2.0.

Madrid Barajas International Airport is bombed. ETA claims responsibility.

2007
At a Glance

World GDP: $55.8tn
  US: $14tn
  Japan: $4.3tn
  China: $3.5tn

World population: 6.62bn

Natural disasters:
  600 die in an earthquake in Peru
  10,000 die in Cyclone Sidr in Bangladesh
  Over 44 die across 20 countries in Western Europe in storms
    caused by Hurricane Kyrill
  Over 20 die in tornadoes across the Southern United States
  Greensburg, Kansas, is almost completely destroyed by a tornado
  9 die in storms and flooding in Newcastle, New South Wales,
    Australia
  Over 200 structures are destroyed in the first 48 hours of the
    Angora Fire in California
  8 die, 800 are injured, and a nuclear power plant is damaged
    in an earthquake near Japan
  Hurricane Dean hits Costa Maya, Mexico, with winds at 165 mph

US federal debt: $9.007tn
US unemployment: 4.6%

Average oil price: $64.20 per barrel
Annual food price index (2002–2004=100): 158.6

World military spending: $1.214tn
  US: $547bn
  UK: $59.7bn
  China: $58.3bn (estimated)
US share of total military spending: 45.1%

Time magazine person of the year: Vladimir Putin

Nobel Peace Prize winners: Intergovernmental Panel on Climate Change and Al Gore Jr., "for their efforts to build up and disseminate greater knowledge about man-made climate change, and to lay the foundations for the measures that are needed to counteract such change."

Introduction

The recession takes hold of the global village but nobody really notices it yet. The financial sector is keeping its poker face, pretending that everything will sort itself out. Against this background, China begins to emerge as the next superpower.

Apple launches the iPhone, the first smart phone with touchscreen capabilities. It will again change how people communicate.

Lenders begin foreclosure proceedings on 1.3m properties, a 79% increase over 2006.

Mortgage-backed securities, groups of subprime mortgages sold many times over, start losing value.

Between 2006 and 2007 Clayton Holdings, the largest residential loan due diligence and securitization surveillance company, issues 900,000 loan reviews; 54% do not meet their standard.

Bear Stearns tells investors that its hedge funds, which have heavily invested in mortgage-backed securities, have become worthless.

The news comes as a surprise to many on Wall Street. The president of Tavakoli Structured Finance asks in a *New York Times* article, "How did you go from reporting very high returns to suddenly now saying the collateral is worth nothing?"

Bear Stearns stock declines to $134 per share, down 14% for the year, yet it is still very high and looking healthy.

Credit default swaps (CDS), insurance on the bankruptcy of giants such as Bear Stearns, are the fastest growing segment of international finance. CDS global volume ranges from $45tn to $62tn.

Moody's increases the ratings of Icelandic investment banks to the highest possible grade: AAA.

The World Fact Book publishes estimates for per capita GDP for the year 2006. The oil-rich United Arab Emirates: $49,700, Norway: $47,800, Ireland: $43,600, the US: $43,500, Iceland: $38,100, Denmark: $37,000, Canada: $35,200, and Austria: $34,100.

Income distribution shows a different picture: in the US, 1% of the population owns 45% of the nation's wealth. Except in the Scandinavian countries, globalization has boosted inequality in the West.

Russia sets aside $3.5bn to address poor health and low life-expectancy: age 60 for men and 72 for women, rather than around 80 for some industrialized countries.

Drinking, smoking, and pollution are said to account for much of the ill-health. Russia's population dropped by 560,000 people in the previous year.

Egypt puts on trial a blogger, Abdel Kareem Nabil, for insulting Islam and causing sectarian strife.

He is reported by the Associated Press as having "often denounced Islamic authorities." The Associated Press adds, "Egypt has arrested a string of pro-democracy bloggers over the past year."

Sweden extends broadband Internet service to areas in its north where there are only three persons per square kilometer.

The BBC reports that as life becomes increasingly hard, many Algerians are turning to a "stricter form of Islam" while not supporting Islamist militants, whom they blame for having traumatized the population.

Algerian jihadists rename themselves "al-Qaeda in the Islamic Maghreb."

Three terrorists suspected to be a part of al-Qaeda are arrested in Germany after allegedly planning attacks on both the Frankfurt International Airport and US military installations.

Bulgaria and Romania officially join the EU. Bulgarian, Romanian, and Irish become official languages of the EU, joining 20 other languages.

The Schengen Agreement area widens, adding nine new countries: the Czech Republic, Estonia, Hungary, Latvia, Lithuania, Malta, Poland, Slovakia, and Slovenia.

Leaders of Hamas and Fatah agree to end hostilities in a meeting in Mecca. Together they form the Palestinian Authority National Unity Government, but tension persists.

The US continues to fund Palestinian Authority President Mahmoud Abbas and his party, Fatah, by sending an $84m aid package largely aimed at improving the fighting ability of the secular group.

Israel releases $100m in frozen assets to Mahmoud Abbas to strengthen the president's position vis-à-vis the democratically elected Hamas.

"They want to see Hamas removed from office and see Fatah in control of everything" said Mouin Rabbani, of the International Crisis Group.

Journalist David Rose reveals that the US and Israel had been actively promoting a coup d'état against Hamas. In July 2007, David Wurmser, Vice President Dick Cheney's chief Middle East adviser, resigns because of this accusation.

Wurmser accuses the White House of "engaging in a dirty war." "There is a stunning disconnect between the president's call for Middle East democracy and this policy," he said. "It directly contradicts it."

Following Fatah's failed attempt to regain power, Hamas attacks Fatah and the Battle of Gaza commences.

Between June 7–15, 2007, Fatah and Hamas fight against each other for control of the Gaza Strip. The International Committee of the Red Cross estimates that 118 people are killed and over 500 injured during the conflict.

Some 6,000 Palestinians flee toward Egypt to find the border at Rafah closed.

Mahmoud Abbas announces the dissolution of the unity government while Hamas declares the end of Western-backed rule in the Gaza Strip.

A Hamas fighter jokes in front of a camera and stages a fake phone call to Secretary of State Condoleezza Rice: "Hello, Condoleezza Rice. You have to deal with me now, there is no Abbas anymore."

In November, Fatah organizes the biggest demonstration in Gaza since Hamas took control in memory of Yasser Arafat. Hamas gunmen disperse a crowd of 200,000.

Trains from North and South Korea cross the 38th Parallel in a test-run agreed to by both governments. This is the first time either side has crossed the Demilitarized Zone since 1953.

President Roh Moo-hyun of South Korea walks across the Military Demarcation Line into North Korea on his way to the second Inter-Korean Summit with North Korean leader Kim Jong Il.

It comes to light that thousands of people, including children, in China's Shanxi province are forced to work in brickyards. The laborers, who are essentially slave labor, have been sold to companies by traffickers.

A UN Environmental Programme report on the environmental consequences of the 2006 war between Lebanon and Israel proves that Israel has been shelling Lebanon with white phosphor.

On March 8, Israeli Prime Minister Ehud Olmert admits that Israel had planned an attack on Lebanon months before the war in 2006.

Olmert visits Jericho. In doing so he becomes the first prime minister to visit the West Bank or Gaza Strip in over seven years.

Israeli airplanes attack and destroy a presumed nuclear facility inside Syria.

The US Justice Department releases an internal audit that proves that the Federal Bureau of Investigation has illegally used the US PATRIOT Act to obtain personal information about US citizens.

In 2007, the situation in Iraq deteriorates further, and Sunni and Shia Muslims begin fighting each other. To avoid the expression "civil war," US officials talk of "ethno-sectarian violence."

The US begins its "surge" into Iraq, adding 28,000 soldiers to its contingent.

The British think-tank Chatham House describes the Iraqi government as largely powerless and irrelevant. It says, "Military force in the form of surges cannot deliver the critical political accommodation."

President Bush addresses the nation at the beginning of the fifth year of Operation Iraqi Freedom. "At this point in the war, our most important mission is helping the Iraqis secure their capital."

In Nisoor Square, Baghdad, Blackwater mercenaries escorting a convoy of the US State Department kill 17 Iraqi civilians.

The next day Blackwater's license to operate in Iraq is temporarily suspended.

The Associated Press reveals it took two weeks for the Americans to start a formal investigation, which discovered that 14 of the shootings were unjustified.

Following this incident and mounting criticism, Blackwater changed its company name to Xe Services. Even with a suspended license, they continued operating in Iraq.

Democracy Now! hosts the father of a nine-year-old child killed in the shooting. He recalls that a Blackwater mercenary kept on shooting at people while his colleagues called for a cease-fire.

A Baghdad market bombing kills at least 135 people and injures a further 339.

On August 14, several car bombs detonate in the Kurdish town of Kahtaniya.

Jeremy Bowen of the BBC asks a senior security official from Saudi Arabia whether the US military presence in Iraq has become "a recruiting ground for Islamist extremists."

His answer: "It inspires these people. Some of them think it is their duty to go and perform jihad in Iraq. They think they are supporting the Muslims in Iraq and actually protecting the Islamic civilization and culture in Iraq."

King Abdullah of Saudi Arabia describes the US military in Iraq as an illegitimate foreign occupation. A friend of the Bush family, on April 17 he declines to attend a state dinner in Washington DC.

In a poll by ABC News, *USA Today*, and others, 51% of Iraqis say violence against US forces is acceptable, and 80% oppose the presence of the US in their country.

Senator James Webb of Virginia expresses his opinion that the US military on the streets in Iraq is an "aggravation," and that it would be better for Iraq that they not be there. Webb is an aggressive former Marine and was Secretary of the Navy during the Reagan administration.

In Yemen, water is scarce. 40% of irrigation water goes to grow the drug khat, widely used by Yemenis, with farmers receiving 20 times the return they would growing potatoes.

Yemen is predominately Muslim, one of the poorest countries in the world, and imports most of its food. Khat gives people who chew it a mild euphoria.

In Bolivia, indigenous people speak of institutions that were closed to them now having open doors because, they say, of President Morales, whom they describe as "one of us."

Some among Bolivia's upper or middle classes complain that Morales is drifting toward totalitarianism and is in tune with the anti-Americanism of his friend, President Hugo Chavez of Venezuela.

Colombian cocaine now travels via Venezuela; in three years, transshipment of drugs has risen by 400%.

In Egypt, it is official: candidates of the ruling party have won 69 of 71 contested seats on the Shura Council, the upper house of Egypt's parliament.

On voting day, police block people from voting and arrest 400 members of the Muslim Brotherhood. The Brotherhood wins no seats and claims it has been cheated.

The Shura Council has 264 members and the ruling party's Hosni Mubarak appoints 88 of them.

The US repeatedly accuses Iran of arming and training Shia Muslims in Iraq. News reports reveal that the US is arming Sunni groups to fight other militant groups.

The Iranian Navy seizes British Royal Navy personnel in Basra. The British claim to be in Iraqi waters and Iran claims they are in Iranian waters.

A few days later, the Iranian president releases them.

The first high-level diplomacy between the US and Iran in 27 years takes place at the home of Iraqi Prime Minister Maliki in Baghdad's Green Zone.

The two sides express interest in a secure and stable Iraq. The Iranians describe the US military in Iraq as an occupation and its effort to train and equip Iraq's security forces as inadequate. They propose a mechanism for coordinating efforts toward Iraqi security.

CBS News reports on a "suicide epidemic" among veterans who served in the US armed forces. In 2005 alone, 6,256 veterans committed suicide.

"It can be tempting to think that America can put aside the burdens of freedom. Yet times of testing reveal the character of a nation," says Bush. "We can, and we will, prevail."

Britain's Royal Society publishes a study that concludes that, on the Atlantic Ocean, hurricanes doubled in frequency in the last century as a result of warmer water surfaces and climate change.

The UN Intergovernmental Panel on Climate Change releases its fourth report concluding that global climate change is "very likely" caused by humans.

The Asia-Pacific Economic Cooperation meeting leads to the signing of a declaration on climate change.

Australian newspaper *The Age* quotes Australian foreign minister Alexander Downer saying, "This is the first occasion ever that China . . . has agreed to any notion of targets at all for developing countries as well as developed countries."

On March 31, the first Earth Hour takes place in Sydney and soon becomes a global phenomenon.

On August 15, an earthquake hits Peru, killing over 500 people.

Michael Moore's documentary *Sicko*, about the American healthcare system, opens in cinemas. The movie fuels the discussion about a national healthcare plan.

China executes Zheng Xiaoyu, convicted of taking bribes to approve medicines that killed an unknown number of people.

Prices on China's stock market rise 130% in 2006 and another 12% into February of 2008, growing 12 times faster than its economic growth.

Concern that China's government will intervene to stop a growing bubble of get-rich enthusiasm sends China's stock prices falling, down 8.8%.

The Shanghai Stock Exchange falls 9%, the largest drop in 10 years. Stock prices drop elsewhere in the world; in the US, 4.3%.

Some people believe that a 10% drop in stock prices in China is an expected "correction" after a long period of rise in the price-value of stocks.

The private equity firm Bain Capital wants to buy the American company 3Com Corp. The purchase would allow the Chinese telecom company Huawei Technologies to control 16.5% of the stocks in 3Com.

The purchase falls through: the US government rules against it on the grounds that 3Com supplied US agencies with network and computer safety products.

In 2007, several new books and news reports cover the growing acquisitions of Chinese companies in Africa. For several years the Chinese companies have pursued an expansionist policy toward African countries, but this process has largely gone unnoticed by the media.

The Chinese expansion generally offers African leaders better terms than their Western competitors, allowing the African nations to press the IMF and Western companies for better conditions in negotiations.

Western attitudes remain negative toward this development. Seeing their former colonies and domains of interest directing their business toward China makes Western leaders uneasy.

"Western countries also buy oil, and have mines around the world. People don't talk about 'grabbing' or 'new colonialism' there. So why is it different for Chinese?" Xu Jianwen, a Chinese person working in Africa, told a *Guardian* reporter.

In Baghdad, both Sunnis and Shia celebrate (by firing weapons into the air) the victory of Shada Hassoun, 25, an Iraqi singer who wins a popular TV talent final staged in Lebanon.

Conservative leader Nikolas Sarkozy wins the French presidential election. In the UK, Gordon Brown replaces Tony Blair as head of the Labour Party and prime minister.

In a report on India's economy, the OECD makes the bold assessment that in 2006 it was the third largest economy, overtaking Germany, France, Italy, Brazil, Japan, and the United Kingdom.

The US and India reach an accord on civilian nuclear power that enables India to buy nuclear fuel from the US India has not signed the Non-Proliferation Treaty (NPT).

Benazir Bhutto returns to Pakistan after eight years in exile. Her return coincides with a court case that challenges Pervez Musharraf's being both president and head of the military.

Before the ruling, Musharraf declares a state of emergency and fires several judges. The newly structured Supreme Court rejects the case against the president.

However, Musharraf steps down as head of the military and is sworn in as a civilian president for his third term in office.

In a campaign rally, a bomb kills Benazir Bhutto.

In an open-hearted conversation with his American colleague, France's ambassador to Tunisia, Serge Degallaix, states: "Tunisia is not a dictatorship" and corruption in the country is not as bad as many places, although Degallaix has concerns about it.

In Argentina, Cristina Fernandez de Kirchner, the wife of former President Néstor Kirchner, becomes elected the first Argentinean woman president.

The "Mitchell Report" is publicly released listing the names of 89 Major League Baseball players that have presumably used anabolic steroids and human growth hormones. Notable players that are named include Roger Clemens and Miguel Tejada.

The Brazilian Military Police invade the favelas of Complexo do Alemão in an episode remembered as the Complexo do Alemão massacre.

A suicide bomber kills at least 50 people in Mazari Sharif, Afghanistan.

The charity event Live Earth organizes worldwide concerts to raise awareness of climate change issues.

An EU special investigation reveals that, until 2007, the CIA has carried out 1,245 "extraordinary renditions."

During the summer of 2007, the CIA releases the "family jewels": nearly 700 pages of documentation of some of the agency's most infamous and illegal operations dating from the 1950s to the 1970s.

The documents include assassination plots against Fidel Castro and Patrice Lumumba, drug tests on unwitting citizens, wiretapping of US journalists, spying on activists, and more.

Operation Banner, the presence of the British Army in Northern Ireland, and the longest-running British Army operation ever, comes to an end.

In the fall of 2007, antigovernment protests in Burma explode. The government eventually cracks down on the protests with brute force.

Buddhist monks join antigovernment protesters in Burma, starting what some called the Saffron Revolution.

Around the world, "volunteers using Facebook" organize protests in support of the Burmese protesters, showing "the increasing power and reach of a social-networking site originally designed to help college students find drinking buddies," reports *Wired* magazine.

A US National Intelligence Estimate states "with high confidence" that Iran froze its nuclear weapons program in 2003. The report contradicts one written in 2005 that stated Iran was determined to continue developing such weapons.

In the US, the Dow Jones Industrial Average reaches a high of a little over 14,000, a sign that credit trouble is being ignored.

In the *New York Times*, David Kelly, an economist at Putnam Investments, is quoted as saying, "If it ain't broke, don't fix it. The American economy is basically strong enough right now to weather the housing downtrend. The Federal Reserve doesn't need to do anything else."

The United Nations Food and Agricultural Organization warns that a 40% rise in food prices in the past year is creating a crisis in poorer countries. The rising prices are attributed to climate change, rising oil prices, and demand for bio-fuels.

Apple's CEO Steve Jobs announces that the company is planning to launch a mobile device that could integrate phone, music, and web capabilities: the iPhone.

"In 2001 we introduced the first iPod, and it didn't just change the way we listen to music, it changed the entire music industry," he says. "Today we're introducing three revolutionary products in this class: an iPod, a phone, and an Internet device."

The iPhone is the first phone that promotes touchscreen technology.

The iPhone goes on sale in the US in June and thousands of people wait in line to get their hands on it. To be the first in line, you would have to wait 109 hours, the *Guardian* reports.

A survey reveals that 6 out of 10 Americans knew the iPhone release date, compared with 2 out of 10 who were able to locate Israel on a map.

"This is the next step in convergence," says Ryan Block, editor of web magazine Engadget.com. "It is taking what is already out there and making it useable for ordinary human beings."

The OECD reports that the average citizen among its member countries disposed of an average of 570 kg of municipal waste in 2007.

Over the summer, all markets are affected by "a combination of growing concerns about the valuation of complex products, liquidity risk, and counter party risk," according to the Bank for International Settlements.

Northern Rock, a bank that relies heavily on short-term funding, seeks support from the Bank of England.

The following morning retail depositors start lining up outside Northern Rock's offices. The bank will later be nationalized.

Major international banks start to write down mortgage related securities.

According to the Bank for International Settlement, at the end of 2007 the nominal value of all outstanding contracts of over-the-counter financial products reaches $600tn, 11 times the world output.

2008
At a Glance

World GDP: $61.8tn
  US: $14.3tn
  Japan: $4.8tn
  China: $4.5tn

World population: 6.697bn

Natural disasters:
- Over 100 die and hundreds of thousands are delayed in snow-storms in China
- Nearly 70,000 die in an earthquake in Sichuan, China
- Nearly 60 die in tornadoes in the Southern US
- Nearly 80,000 die in Cyclone Nargis in Burma
- 12 die and hundreds are injured in an earthquake in northern Japan
- Over 1,000 die when Typhoon Fengshen hits the Philippines
- Hundreds die in Hurricane Hanna, mainly in Haiti
- Nearly 200 die in Hurricane Ike in Haiti; it also causes devastation in Louisiana and Texas
- Nearly 70 die in Typhoon Hagupit in the Phillipines, China, Taiwan, and Vietnam
- Over 100 die and nearly 80,000 are evacuated from the Santa Catarina floods in Brazil
- Over 4,500 evacuate when Chaiten Volcano erupts in Chile

US federal debt: $10.024tn
US unemployment: 5.8%

Average oil price: $91.48 per barrel
Annual food price index (2002–2004=100): 199.6

World military spending: $1.464tn
  US: $607bn
  China: $84.9bn (estimated)
  France: $65.7bn
US share of total military spending: 41.5%

Time magazine person of the year: Barack Obama

Nobel Peace Prize winner: Martti Ahtisaari "for his important efforts, on several continents and over more than three decades, to resolve international conflicts."

Introduction

2008 is the year when greed is no longer a positive goal. The collapse of Lehman Brothers exposes the fragility of the financial system, centered around scams and the inability of the political and international institutions to regulate the economy. Anarchy rules the markets.

Against this backdrop, Barack Obama embraces the digital revolution, utilizing the Internet as the most powerful tool of his campaign.

Oil prices hit $100 per barrel for the first time ever.

"Traders who are skittish about the weakening dollar and fallout from the American credit crisis regard oil as a safe haven," writes the *New York Times*.

Michael Greenberger, former director of Trading and Markets at the Commodity Futures Trading Commission, testifies before Congress, stating, "Investment banks are prime players in the crude oil future markets."

"The futures trading done by those institutions are executed through subsidiaries neither registered with the banking regulators nor with the [Securities and Exchange Commission]," resulting in "haphazard, incomplete, and unaudited" data and no regulation.

"By any objective assessment, the crude oil market is now overwhelmingly dominated by speculation," Greenberger continued.

After a week of optimism, Wall Street takes another hit: the Dow drops almost 3%. On the New York Mercantile Exchange, gold prices hit $1,000 an ounce for the first time ever.

Banks are the big losers. They have financed their long-term investments by borrowing short-term, creating an enormous mismatch. Losses have been moved out of the balance sheet.

The British Government passes emergency legislation to nationalize Northern Rock, the 5th largest mortgage bank in the UK.

Stock market guru Jim Cramer shouts, "No! No! No! Bear Stearns is not in trouble. . . . Don't move your money from Bear," after shares went from $68 to $30 in four days.

A few days later, Bear Stearns, a highly leveraged investment bank with large mortgage exposure, is short of cash and risks bankruptcy.

To save the bank, Treasury Secretary Hank Paulson convinces JPMorgan Chase to buy Bear Stearns stocks. Paulson promises $30bn to guarantee the solvency of Bear Stearns.

Chase offers to buy it at $4 per share. Paulson reduces the price to $2 per share to avoid rewarding Bear Stearns. Employees at Bear Stearns are in shock.

Wall Street fails to make the connection between the meltdown at Bear Stearns and the health of the economy.

Due to huge liquidity problems, the US government nationalizes Fannie Mae and Freddie Mac, companies that had securitized the bulk of US mortgages.

It is the biggest nationalization in US history, since the nominal value of mortgages held or guaranteed by Fannie Mae and Freddie Mac is $5.3tn, close to 40% of US GDP.

The Fed also announces that it will buy $500bn of mortgage-backed securities issued by Fannie and Freddie to prevent people from becoming homeless.

As home prices drop 20% from their peak in 2006, foreclosures increase by 81% from 2007. In early 2008, the delinquency rate on mortgage payments skyrockets to 25%.

US private debt, which amounted to 123% of GDP in 1981, reaches 290% by the third quarter of 2008.

A 2008 OECD report on the US economy states, "The federal government budget is far from being on a sustainable path," and among the population, inequality is rising.

Income inequality becomes a topic of debate. Paul Krugman writes about how during the last two decades the income gap has widened.

In the 1970s a CEO was paid roughly 40 times as much as the average worker. By the beginning of the 21st century, however, CEOs were making 367 times the salary of an average worker.

The financial institution Merrill Lynch sells itself to Bank of America.

On September 15, 2008, Lehman Brothers files for bankruptcy protection. The event marks a milestone in the early stages of the financial crises.

On the morning of its bankruptcy, Lehman was still rated "investment grade" from major rating agencies.

The Lehman bankruptcy sparks fear across the globe. Financial institutions are on the brink of collapse and governments take over their debts in an attempt to prevent further catastrophic collapses.

The idea of "too big to fail" is applied all over the world. It introduces the concept that major banks are of systemic importance to the global financial market, and their collapse could bring down the entire world economy.

The stock price of American International Group (AIG), the biggest insurance company in the world with $1tn in assets, falls by 90%. In previous years, AIG had issued $3.2tn of credit default swaps for Lehman Brothers.

The Fed organizes AIG's bailout in exchange for 80% of AIG's equity. The deal, a sort of nationalization, is worth $150bn.

It slowly becomes clear that the so-called "masters of Wall Street" had not understood the risk profiles of financial instruments.

Meanwhile, Goldman Sachs and Morgan Stanley request the Fed to let them become commercial banks. The Fed approves the transformation. As of autumn 2008, there are no more stand-alone investment banks in the US.

President Bush signs an emergency bailout package allowing the government to purchase failing bank assets. The $700bn package, known as the Troubled Asset Relief Program (TARP), is utilized to inject money into troubled banks.

The British Government infuses £37bn ($64bn) of new capital into the Royal Bank of Scotland, Lloyds, and HBOS, to avert a financial sector collapse.

March 19: "Bloody Friday" sees many of the world's stock exchanges experience their worst decline in history, with drops of around 10%.

Critical failures in the US financial system begin to build up after mid-September, and the Dow Jones Industrial Average reaches its lowest level since 1997.

One of the first sectors to be hit by the financial crisis is the technology sector. eBay cuts 10% of its workforce a month after Lehman collapses, while Google and Microsoft shares plummet.

Bill Gates, while announcing a plan to acquire Yahoo!, declares that he will retire after 33 years as the head of Microsoft. "We've really achieved the ideal of what I wanted Microsoft to become," he states.

Lady Gaga releases her first album, *The Fame*, with hit songs like "Poker Face" and "Just Dance."

In the words of *Rolling Stone* magazine: "Here was a New York art diva who knew how to make a spectacle of herself, . . . storming the Top 40 with the battle cry, 'This beat is sick/I wanna take a ride on a disco stick!'"

The pop icon comments, "I feel freer in underwear, and I fucking hate pants."

The music distribution service Spotify is released in Western Europe. The company allows members to listen to a nearly endless supply of music for a monthly fee.

Bernard Madoff is arrested in New York on fraud charges. His wealth management company is shown to be a large ponzi scheme. In newspapers around the world, people relish accounts of his lifestyle of excess.

The story is irresistible to media as many of his clients are celebrities. Madoff is sentenced to 150 years in prison for fraud and money laundering the next year.

In a report on Latin American economies, the OECD stresses the importance of a strong performing fiscal policy, especially as the continent is largely in the midst of democratic consolidation.

The Union of South American Nations (UNASUR) signs a constitutive treaty that, when ratified, will establish the union as a legal entity, forming a stronger union between nations in South America.

The OECD's strong emphasis on government as a force for development is a shift from previous beliefs in neo-liberal economic policies that had been dogmatic on the continent.

Developing countries break the record for providing net financial resources to developed countries. The new high is $933bn.

In Europe, one of the countries worst hit by the financial crisis is the little island of Iceland. The Icelandic government takes control of three banks.

It's revealed that 80% of Icelandic foreign debt, amounting to $50bn, is held by its banks.

Six central banks announce jointly that they will reduce interest rates by 50 basis points. This is the first time central banks of Europe and North America make a joint statement.

The Fed reduces the Federal Fund rate to 0+. Other rate reductions are no longer possible, thus the Fed begins to use a policy called quantitative easing (QE).

QE increases the supply of money in the economy by, among other things, buying bonds and hence reducing interest rates. This gives consumers more money to spend.

President Bush announces the government will loan $17.4bn to General Motors and Chrysler.

In a special issue, the *Economist* warns about US indebtedness: "Between 2000 and 2008 the country received over $5.7 trillion from abroad to invest, equivalent to over 40% of its 2007 GDP."

In early 2008, leading economists Joseph Stiglitz and Linda J. Bilmes publish their estimations of the cost of the US war in Iraq: $3tn. The Bush administration's estimates in 2003 had been around $50-60bn.

Fox News, among others, reports that a Pentagon study has found no link between Saddam Hussein and al-Qaeda. The study is based on more than 600,000 Iraqi documents seized after the invasion of Iraq.

A Human Rights Watch report states that the majority of detainees in Guantánamo spend 22 hours a day alone in small cells with little or no natural light or fresh air.

None of these prisoners has ever been allowed a visit from a family member, and most of them have never been allowed to make a single phone call during their imprisonment.

Detainees' repeated hunger strikes and suicide attempts are seen by the US military as a challenge to its authority, Human Rights Watch continues.

In July 2008, Seymour Hersh reveals in an article in the *New Yorker* that the US had been plotting a war against Iran for some time. In 2007, the Democrat-controlled US Congress had approved funding for a major escalation of covert operations in Iran.

In a meeting with President Ben Ali of Tunisia, the US embassy asks Ali to assist the US in improving relations with Libya. At the meeting Ali predicts that the situation in the region is "explosive," especially in Egypt, but Yemen and Saudi Arabia also face real troubles.

"Riots from Haiti to Bangladesh to Egypt over the soaring costs of basic foods have brought the issue to a boiling point and catapulted it to the forefront of the world's attention," CNN reports.

"This is the world's big story," Jeffrey Sachs, director of Columbia University's Earth Institute, comments about the riots.

The manifesto Charter 08 is signed by over 300 intellectuals and activists in China. One of the authors is Liu Xiaobo.

The manifesto calls for reforms of the political and judicial institutions and strengthened civil rights legislation.

In the run-up to the opening ceremony of the Beijing Olympic games, the "torch around the world" is attacked in attempts to criticize China for its civil rights record. Inside China, the protests are widely seen as an attack on China and the Chinese people.

The melamine scandal emerges in China. Eggs and milk have been contaminated with melamine, causing the death of at least six infants and harming many more. The Chinese, lacking tight regulations and supervision of safety precautions, are at constant risk for such scandal.

Throughout the decade, reports of products from China containing high levels of hazardous substances are recurring. News reports of high lead content in toys surface on a regular basis.

An earthquake hits the province of Sichuan in China. Nearly 70,000 people lose their lives in the earthquake and millions are left homeless.

Cyclone Nargis kills over 100,000 people in Burma.

Former Prime Minister of Thailand Thaksin Shinawatra is arrested on corruption charges upon returning to Thailand after months of exile.

Thailand enters turbulent political times with strong antigovernment demonstrations; a state of emergency is called and a constitutional court ruling forces Prime Minister Samak Sundaravej to resign after hosting a cooking show.

President Pervez Musharraf's party suffers a big defeat in Pakistan's general elections.

Pakistan-based terrorists kill 164 and injure more than 250 people in Mumbai, India, in a series of coordinated attacks against the Taj Mahal and Oberoi hotels.

Musharraf resigns under impeachment pressure for failing to step down after losing the election earlier in the year.

The movie *Slumdog Millionaire* charms the world. It will win eight Oscars at the academy awards in 2009.

Raul Castro assumes the presidency in Cuba after Fidel Castro, his brother, resigns.

Luis Moreno-Ocampo, prosecutor of the International Criminal Court, charges Sudan's president, Omar Hassan al-Bashir, with genocide for planning and executing the killing of Darfur's main ethnic tribes.

Robert Mugabe is reelected in the Zimbabwean presidential election with over 85% of the votes. The election and its dubious circumstances are given widespread attention in Western media.

Due to international pressure, Mugabe is forced to negotiate a power-sharing deal with opposition leader Morgan Tsvangirai later in the year.

Dimitri Medvedev becomes president of Russia; however, Vladimir Putin remains a powerful figure in Russian politics.

Russia invades Georgia, claiming to liberate the area of South Ossetia, and recognizes South Ossetia and Abkhazia as independent entities.

In the US, John McCain and Barack Obama battle to become president of the United States.

Obama uses the Internet and social networks to convince young people to vote for him. Obama "rocked the youth vote," according to the *Guardian*, by using the web. Obama wins 70% of the vote among young Americans under 25.

He raises $160m through online fundraising, with individuals giving up to $200 each.

Obama's slogan, "Yes, we can," inspires people's hope for a better future after eight years of President Bush.

In Europe, people are enthusiastic about him and political leaders from all sides try to assert themselves as "friends of Obama."

California legalizes same-sex marriage after the state's own Supreme Court rules a previous ban unconstitutional.

Australian Prime Minister Kevin Rudd apologizes to the country's indigenous population for past abductions and oppression.

Similarly, the Canadian government apologizes to its indigenous population for abductions and abuses.

The world is in the grip of vampire fever. It starts with the movie *Twilight*, which is followed by the sequels *New Moon* and *Eclipse*.

Located underneath the Swiss mountains, scientists complete the Large Hadron Collider, a 17-mile-long looped track that will enable scientists to accelerate particles and smash them together to understand how matter formed at the beginning of the universe.

After being held by the Revolutionary Armed Forces of Colombia (FARC) for over six years, Colombian politician Ingrid Betancourt is freed along with 15 other hostages.

Ireland votes to reject the EU Lisbon treaty. The treaty was to be the basis for stronger cooperation within the EU.

From July 8–10, the G8 meets in Hokkaido, Japan.

Several trade ships are hijacked by pirates outside the coast of Somalia.

In the turbulent 1990s, tons of Western chemical and radioactive waste was dumped in Somalia's unguarded waters. At the other end of the long Somalian coast, industrial fishing vessels from the West and the Far East ruined the livelihood of local fishermen.

Local warlords have no trouble finding despaired laborers that have few options but to join the pirates. Western countries react to the pirates by sending war ships to the region.

Thomas Beatie, the world's first pregnant man, gives birth to a daughter.

President George W. Bush makes his fourth and final trip to Iraq as president on December 14. At a press conference, Iraqi journalist Muntadhar al-Zaidi throws his shoes at the president.

Just before the year ends, Israel launches an offensive on the Gaza Strip, starting with extensive waves of airstrikes. The aim of the operation is to stop the launching of rockets into Israel, but the force used triggers international protests.

2009
At a Glance

World GDP: $58.2tn
  US: $14.1tn
  Japan: $5tn
  China: $4.9tn

World population: 6.775bn

Natural disasters:
  Nearly 200 die in bushfires in southeastern Australia
  Nearly 300 die in an earthquake in Italy
  Over 1,000 die in Typhoon Morakot in Taiwan
  Hundreds die in Typhoon Ketsana in the Philippines and Vietnam
  Nearly 200 die in a tsunami triggered by an earthquake near the Samoan islands
  Over 1,000 die in an earthquake in Sumatra, Indonesia
  An earthquake hits Costa Rica
  Mount Redoubt, a volcano in Alaska, begins to erupt after a prolonged period of unrest
  An earthquake hits 160 km west of Invercargill, New Zealand, creating a small tsunami

US federal debt: $11.909tn
US unemployment: 9.27%

Average oil price: $53.48 per barrel
Annual food price index (2002–2004=100): 156.8

World military spending: $1.531tn
  US: $661bn
  China: $100bn (estimated)
  France: $63.9bn
US share of total military spending: 43.2%

Time magazine person of the year: Ben Bernanke

Nobel Peace Prize winner: Barack Obama "for his extraordinary efforts to strengthen international diplomacy and cooperation between peoples."

Introduction

Barack Obama, the president of hope, enters the White House. Seldom have so many expectations been placed on one president to change things back to the way they were, before Bush and the neo-cons attempted to draw a new world order.

On the other side of the world in Iran and China, the civil society empowered by Twitter and other social media attempts the impossible: to change the status quo.

As newly elected President Obama moves into the White House, the economy is at the top of his agenda.

He appoints Timothy Geithner, former head of the New York Fed, as treasury secretary and confirms Ben Bernanke for a second term as chair of the Fed.

Obama then appoints Larry Summers director of the National Economic Council.

One of the new president's election promises is to regulate the banking sector, seen by many on Main Street as the cause of the economic crisis.

"It's a Wall Street government," says Robert Gnaizda, former director of the Greenlining Institute.

"The turmoil is the product of a global credit boom, characterized by a broad underpricing of risk, excessive leverage by financial institutions, and an increasing reliance on complex and opaque financial instruments that have proven to be fragile under stress," acknowledges Ben Bernanke.

The blame falls on Wall Street rating agencies: they did not ring any bells about banks' insolvencies.

Dagong Global Credit Rating, the Chinese rating agency, comes out of the crisis as a reputable institution, rivaling US-based Standard & Poor's and Moody's.

Iceland's banking system collapses and Prime Minister Geir Haarde resigns. With a foreign debt 10 times the GDP, the Icelandic economy is in free fall.

The *Guardian* says that Haarde has "the dubious distinction of being the first world leader to leave office as a direct result of the world financial crisis."

Jóhanna Sigurðardóttir replaces Haarde as prime minister. She is the world's first openly lesbian head of government.

The delinquency rate on US mortgages continues to rise and reaches a staggering 14.4%.

To counteract the credit crunch, the US, UK, and Western European governments offer a $9tn credit line to banks in trouble using taxpayers' money.

Martin Wolf, columnist of the *Financial Times*, comments, "The balance sheet of the state was put behind the banks."

The impact of the crisis moves from the private sector to nations.

Wolf underlines the lack of regulation and the ability of banks to use "off-balance-sheet vehicles, the derivatives, and the 'shadow banking system' itself . . . to find a way round regulation."

Tommaso Padoa-Schioppa, former Italian treasury minister, publishes an analysis of the crisis entitled *The Short View*, stressing that "growth without saving" cannot be sustained.

Growth in the early 2000s was artificial since it was fuelled by "economic imbalances" unsustainable in the long term.

Chinese and Indian surpluses counterbalance huge commercial deficits in the US and Western countries.

Padoa-Schioppa also emphasizes the disadvantages and risks of having prolonged low interest rates in Western countries.

The Bank for International Settlements reports that policies adopted after the tech bubble of the early 2000s led to "taking on more risk" and "too much confidence."

Barry Eichengreen, an American economist, writes that these policies "seduced business in general, and financial business in particular, into believing that it was safe to use more leverage and to invest in more volatile assets."

In Britain, expenses from members of Parliament are leaked to the *Daily Telegraph* and published, uncovering a vast misuse of public money.

Politicians are forced to resign amid public outcry.

After being bailed out by the US government, AIG announces it will pay its top executives $165m in bonuses. Both Democrats and Republicans are shocked and angered by the announcement.

Bernanke declares, "It makes me angry." Andrew Cuomo, New York attorney general, launches an investigation into AIG bonuses.

General Motors files for Chapter 11 bankruptcy. It is the fourth largest US bankruptcy in history.

General Motors puts Opel, and Saab up for sale, and Ford tries to unload Volvo. In Germany the Opel deal becomes a political football with bidders from China and Russia.

GM decides to keep Opel but Saab is sold to a sports cars manufacturer and Volvo to the Geely group, a Chinese company.

Demonstrations are held across the Western world against bankers and regulators and their lack of oversight.

In London, a mass protest is organized during the G20 summit under the slogan "Put People First."

According to the US National Bureau of Economic Research, the Great Recession started in December 2007 and ends in June 2009.

In the US and Western Europe, the projected recovery is very mild with average growth at around 0.3%.

The US unemployment rate reaches 10.1%; Western Europe experiences a similar hike. For the first time, younger generations won't be wealthier than their parents.

In California, Governor Arnold Schwarzenegger terminates at least 700,000 jobs as the state approaches bankruptcy.

According to the World Bank, the Arab world, China, Australia, and some South American countries are less affected by the crisis than other regions.

The World Bank issues a report stating that between 1981 and 2004, the number of people living below the poverty line fell by half a billion.

The reduction is entirely due to economic progress in China.

The World Bank concludes that China's progress in poverty reduction over the last 25 years has been enviable, impressive, and remarkable.

With US imports of Chinese goods plummeting during the financial crisis, China turns to its own population to consume more.

The Chinese government injects massive amounts of money into its economy to boost consumption.

It also subsidizes production of environmentally friendly refrigerators, air conditioners, washing machines, etc., in order to increase consumption.

The OECD reports that since 1971, global emissions of carbon dioxide have risen by 99%.

World leaders meet in Copenhagen to seek agreements on how to meet mounting challenges associated with climate change.

On one side the US and the industrialized Western world call for a stronger commitment from China and other developing countries.

On the other side China, India, South Africa, and Brazil argue that the Western world should carry a larger burden for polluting the world in past decades.

The conference is unable to reach agreement on key issues, though it does produce the Copenhagen Accord.

Chinalco, the Chinese-government-owned aluminum company, bids for an 18% stake in the Australian company Rio Tinto. The proposed investment is worth $19.5bn.

Chinalco pressures for the deal to be accepted in a very open way, since the investment would be the largest foreign investment by a Chinese company in the world.

A political debate raising issues over China getting too much influence on the market price of steel leads to the rejection of the offer.

In response to a video allegedly showing Chinese soldiers beating up Tibetan monks, China blocks YouTube.

Over 100 Han Chinese are killed in riots stirred by the minority Uyghur population in the Chinese province of Xinjiang.

The Uyghur population, a Turkic Muslim people, has been discriminated against for a long time; they have not benefitted as much as the Han from the Chinese economic miracle.

Following the riots, China blocks Facebook and Twitter. These websites are still blocked.

In Iran, the presidential election is highly controversial, bringing thousands of people into the streets. Incumbent president Mahmoud Ahmadinejad is reelected with 62% of the vote.

Many inside Iran say that the election was rigged by fraud and take their rage onto the streets of Tehran.

Western governments express deep concern about the vote and the riots in Tehran. US Vice President Joe Biden admits to having an "awful lot of doubt" about the credibility of the election.

Police discover the biggest laboratory for the production of cocaine in Bolivia. The country trails only Peru and Colombia as top producer and exporter of cocaine. Colombia accounts for 54% of worldwide production.

The EU is "concerned about alleged irregularities" in the Iranian election, and Bernard Kouchner, French foreign minister, criticizes the "brutal reactions" against demonstrators.

The Iranian government tries to block the international media from covering the protests but demonstrators broadcast their rage across the world with the help of YouTube, Facebook, and Twitter.

Around the world, individuals help the protesters by providing server space and rerouting Iranian tweets through other countries whose Internet access the Iranian government cannot control.

"Twitter, the Medium of the Movement," reads a *Time* magazine headline.

The US State Department recognizes the importance of Twitter in the Iranian protests and asks Twitter to delay an upgrade in support of protesters.

In a speech in Cairo, Egypt, US President Obama calls for "a new beginning between the United States and Muslims around the world."

The International Criminal Court (ICC) issues an arrest warrant for Sudanese President Omar Hassan al-Bashir for war crimes and crimes against humanity in Darfur.

Al-Bashir is the first sitting head of state to be indicted by the ICC since its establishment in 2002.

Former Peruvian President Alberto Fujimori is sentenced to 25 years in prison for ordering killings and kidnappings of his opponents.

An earthquake hits L'Aquila, Italy. Prime Minister Silvio Berlusconi causes outrage when he says that the homeless victims should consider themselves to be on a "camping weekend."

Berlusconi hosts the G8 at L'Aquila; celebrities flock to the city in ruins but reconstruction proves to be slow and full of problems.

"Shortages of money, political will, architectural good sense, and international attention, along with a distinctly Italian predilection for a kind of magical thinking, threaten to finish what the quake started," writes the *New York Times*.

Bushfires overwhelm southeastern Australia. Drought, extreme temperatures, and terrific wind speeds enable the fire to spread rapidly. An area of roughly 1.1m acres is burned.

The WHO expresses concerns over an influenza virus spreading from Mexico.

Mexico closes down schools and public events, leaving city streets deserted. Several governments act to prevent the spreading of the virus, known as swine flu.

The WHO announces that the world is on the brink of a pandemic, calling for countries to take precautions.

On a trip to Cameroon, the pope proclaims that HIV/AIDS "is a tragedy that cannot be overcome by money alone, that cannot be overcome through the distribution of condoms, which even aggravates the problems."

Sweden legalizes same-sex marriage.

Ireland votes yes to the EU's Lisbon treaty after having voted no the previous year.

After French and Dutch referenda vote against a new European constitution, the EU opts to change the framework with the Lisbon treaty. The treaty goes in effect on December 1, 2009.

Russia and Ukraine argue over the price of gas again.

Russia uses gas exports for foreign policy goals and is less inclined to subsidize gas prices for Ukraine, which has a more pro-Western government.

Russia cuts gas exports to Ukraine, resulting in a shortage of gas for Eastern Europe.

Abdel Basset Ali al-Megrahi, the Libyan terrorist convicted of bombing the PanAm flight that exploded over Lockerbie and killed 270 people in 1988, is freed on compassionate grounds.

Al-Megrahi flies to Libya to receive treatment for terminal prostate cancer. His life expectancy is a few months. To date he is still alive.

WikiLeaks publishes a classified report from the US embassy in Tunis that says that the situation in Tunisia appears to be deteriorating with increasing repression and corruption.

The US, however, cannot "write off Tunisia" as there is "too much at stake," says the report. After all, Tunisia is a friend in the war on terror.

The Nobel Peace Prize is awarded to Barack Obama, despite the ongoing US wars. Obama accepts the prize, saying that the prize, in this case, is awarded to give momentum to a set of causes.

In his first year as president, Barack Obama does not fulfill many of his campaign promises: Guantánamo is still open, healthcare reform is not yet in place, and the Bush tax cuts are not yet repealed.

America and the world wait to see what Obama will do next, finding some comfort in the fact that Obama isn't Bush.

On Independence Day, the Statue of Liberty's crown is reopened to the public after eight years. It was closed for security reasons following the World Trade Center attacks.

Having promised to end the war in Iraq in his campaign, Obama shifts attention to Afghanistan soon after his inauguration.

He doubles US forces in Afghanistan from roughly 30,000 to 60,000.

The Obama administration also boosts the use of drones, unmanned bombers controlled from military bases in the US, which strike in Afghanistan and, increasingly, in Pakistan.

A Pakistani newspaper claims the drones have killed only 14 al-Qaeda leaders and nearly 700 civilians.

An American soldier in Iraq opens fire on a counseling center at Camp Liberty in Baghdad, leaving five soldiers dead and three wounded.

Baghdad is hit by three major bombings that kill over 100 people. The targets include the financial ministry, the justice ministry, Baghdad's provincial administration building, the foreign ministry, a courthouse, two colleges, a mosque, and a bank.

Some of the bombs go off in the supposedly safest areas of the city. "While Baghdad is often hit by attacks, it is unusual for them to penetrate such well-fortified areas of the cities," writes the BBC.

A bomb explodes in Palma Nova, Mallorca, killing two police officers. Basque separatist group ETA is believed to be responsible.

The Jakarta double bombings at the JW Marriott and Ritz-Carlton hotels kill nine people, including four foreigners.

The separatist group Liberation Tigers of Tamil Eelam is defeated after fighting a 25-year civil war with the Sri Lankan government.

The Tamil Tigers originate from the minority Hindu population. President Mahinda Rajapaska proclaims the country "liberated from separatist terror."

The "mopping up" campaign against the separatists costs tens of thousands of civilian lives. Most of them are killed by government shelling.

The Naxalites, a Maoist movement composed of indigenous people in the Eastern part of India, regain strength.

Big business, coupled with oppression from corrupt officials, has taken the land from local people.

In retaliation, the Naxalites ambush government troops, killing at least 76 people. It is the deadliest strike against the government in their 43-year insurgency.

Prime Minister Manmohan Singh goes as far as to say that the Naxalites are the gravest internal security threat to India.

74 people, mostly Army officials, are killed in Pilkhana, Bangladesh. The paramilitary border patrols turn their weapons on the officers in a dispute over pay.

17 people are shot dead in the Winnenden school shooting in Germany.

Internationally renowned journalist Günther Wallraff exposes latent and explicit racism in Germany by working undercover.

Israel attacks Gaza. Shelling from Hamas and air strikes from Israel continue to menace the area, although less frequently.

The UN Fact-Finding Mission on the Gaza Conflict releases the Goldstone Report, named after South African former judge Richard Goldstone, who led the mission.

The report concludes that both Hamas and Israel have violated laws of war, and that Israel has used disproportionate force, targeting civilians.

North Korea announces that it has conducted a successful test of a nuclear bomb.

US Airways Flight 1549 makes an emergency landing into the Hudson River shortly after takeoff from La Guardia Airport in New York City. All passengers and crewmembers survive.

Air France Flight 447 crashes into the Atlantic Ocean off the coast of Brazil on a flight from Rio de Janeiro to Paris. All 228 passengers and crew are killed.

The Washington DC subway crashes: two trains collide killing nine and injuring over 80.

The 72-year run of the American soap opera *Guiding Light* ends as its final episode is broadcast.

Renowned golfer Tiger Woods crashes his car following a domestic dispute. Newspapers dig up several stories of adultery.

Several sponsors abandon Woods, but Accenture initially stands by its superstar with a new billboard that reads "It's what you do next that counts."

Accenture soon changes its mind and cancels its contract with Woods.

The movie *Avatar* revolutionizes the film industry, using a new stereoscopic filming technique and innovative filming technologies to render the movie in 3D.

Michael Jackson dies and makes top newspaper headlines around the world.

Jackson was scheduled for a comeback series of eight concerts in London the same summer, but died from cardiac arrest.

Jackson's physician faces charges for allegedly giving Jackson an overdose of medicine.

Lady Gaga releases her album *The Fame Monster*, including hits like "Bad Romance" and "Telephone."

The international superstar raises eyebrows when attending the 2010 MTV Video awards in a dress made of meat.

Cristiano Ronaldo moves from Manchester United to join Real Madrid for a whopping €94m, making it the most expensive soccer transfer ever.

At the Track and Field World Championships, Usain Bolt sets a new world record for the 100-meter dash, 9.58 seconds, shattering his own previous record.

The men behind the file-sharing website the Pirate Bay are found guilty on charges of assisting copyright infringements.

The Pirate Bay is "one of the world's largest facilitators of illegal downloading," states the *LA Times*, and is a major hub for people wanting to distribute software and computer files.

Copyright infringements have become a major problem for the entertainment industry and lawmakers alike. With the development of torrent technology, file sharing is much easier.

2010
At a Glance

World GDP: $63.0tn
  US: $14.5tn
  China: $5.9tn
  Japan: $5.5tn

World population: 6.884bn

Natural disasters:
  Over 230,000 die in an earthquake in Haiti
  Nearly 500 die in an earthquake in Chile
  Over 2,000 die in an earthquake in Qinghai province in China
  Volcano Eyjafjallajökull erupts disrupting air traffic in Western
     Europe for several weeks
  1,500 die in floods in Pakistan, about 3m are affected
  Over 400 die in a tsunami in Sumatra, Indonesia
  350 die from volcanic eruptions from Mount Merapi in Indonesia
  A handful of people die as toxic sludge floods parts of Hungary

US federal debt: $13.561tn
US unemployment: 9.6%

Average oil price: $71.21 per barrel
Annual food price index (2002–2004=100): 185.1

World military spending: $1.630tn
  US: $698bn
  China: $119bn (estimated)
  UK: $59.6bn
US share of total military spending: 42.8%

Time magazine person of the year: Mark Zuckerberg

Nobel Peace Prize winner: Liu Xiaobo "for his long and non-violent struggle for fundamental human rights in China."

Introduction

While the BRIC countries recover quickly from the financial crisis, Europe gets caught in the sovereign debt storm. Ireland and Greece have to be bailed out. Portugal, Spain, and Italy are next in line.

The fiscal crisis risks breaking up the Eurozone and indeed the whole EU, with resentment rising and the EU's economic locomotive, Germany, having trouble of its own.

But the real problems are political. WikiLeaks exposes the lies and manipulation of Western leaders, their liaisons with the moneyed elites, and the infringement of human rights in Iraq. The launching of the iPad simplifies and speeds up the pace at which this news travels. It is impossible to stop the unveiling of the truth.

After revising the country's finances, Greece's newly elected government announces that the previous administration lied about the size of the debt and deficit.

Foreign investment banks had provided plenty of accounting tricks to "cook the books."

The Greek deficit is revised from 6% to 12.7% of GDP. Markets are in shock.

Greece declares that it will not to be able to honor its forthcoming debt repayments and seeks help from the EU.

To finance its debt, Greece now has to pay three times as much as Germany because the market fears insolvency.

As the economic situation deteriorates in Greece, markets lose confidence in other European countries with equally large deficits: Italy, Ireland, Spain, and Portugal.

Goldman Sachs names these countries PIIGS (including Greece). Market analysts fear that if one defaults all the others will follow suit.

Europe's sovereign debt crisis triggers a debate over the possibility of a break-up of the EU.

Many wonder if the new crisis is linked to the credit crunch, since countries such as Ireland have guaranteed the debt of their banking sectors.

Niall Ferguson, the British financial and economic historian, tells the *Financial Times*, "The sovereign debt crisis is a fiscal crisis of the Western world."

As one the most influential countries in the EU, Germany must play a major role in solving the crisis. German Chancellor Angela Merkel tries to convince the electorate of the necessity to bail out Greece.

Exploiting the situation, populist forces attack Merkel and her party for "not putting Germany first." But she is able to maintain her majority.

Finally, the IMF and the EU agree to a €110bn credit line to save Greece from defaulting on debt repayments. It's "the fattest check in history," laments the German press.

In exchange, Greece must introduce an austerity plan. Violent protests break out in the street against the IMF and the government plan.

"For years now the prime minister of Greece will be [IMF chair] Dominique Strauss-Kahn," comments Dimitrios Papadimoulis, a leftist Greek politician.

Although the PIIGS are at the periphery of the Eurozone, Spain and Italy are big economies. If dragged into the sovereign debt crisis, their insolvency could hurt the EU.

Spain wins the World Cup in South Africa, boosting hopes that this victory will help the Spanish economy to recover.

Ireland is forced to accept help from the IMF and the Eurozone. The banking system in Ireland is crippled by debt.

Some people argue that behind the sovereign debt crisis there are speculators who are getting back the money they have lost in the credit crunch by betting against Europe.

Speculation is indeed rampant about the possibility of default among the PIIGS.

Wen Jiabao, the Chinese premier, announces that China is willing to buy Greek bonds to strengthen the Greek economy.

China is also interested in acquiring Greek ports to facilitate access to the European market.

Cosco, China's state-owned shipping giant, leases Pier Two of the Piraeus port for the next 35 years for close to $5bn.

The Chinese "are not like these Wall Street fucks, pushing financial investments on paper. The Chinese deal in real things," says Theodoros Pangalos, deputy prime minister. The *Economist* writes that buyers based in China or Hong Kong account for a tenth of global deals in value terms.

EU commissioner for industry Antonio Tajani proposes the creation of a new agency to regulate foreign, mainly Chinese, purchases of key European industries.

The G20 summit in South Korea agrees to reform the IMF, shifting more influence from European governments to emerging economies.

The *Washington Post* reports that China has surpassed Japan as the second largest economy in the world.

Shanghai hosts the World Expo. For several months the world gathers in the Chinese metropolis and witnesses China's newly acquired economic status.

China overtakes the US as the largest car market in the world.

"Being able to afford a car in China is not so difficult any more. People with an average salary can afford to buy a car," says Rao Da, secretary general of the China Passenger Car Association.

According to the OECD, urban Chinese households are now well equipped with electrical appliances.

Nearly all urban homes have washing machines, air conditioning units, color TVs, and mobile phones. Ownership of microwave ovens and computers has also spread.

The size of an apartment in urban areas has risen by nearly one-third since the early 2000s, to 700 square feet for the average family of three.

Top Chinese earners are reaching Western standards. "Their average household income level now exceeds that of 30% of US households."

China also pursues a greener industry by setting specific targets for the closure of inefficient energy-intensive industries, and providing funding and tax breaks to upgrade existing industrial infrastructure.

Several workers in the Foxconn factory of Shenzhen, where the iPhone and other electronic products are produced, commit suicide, highlighting China's poor record for workers' rights.

"Suicides at factories in southern China have not been uncommon over the past decade, but in recent years improvements in mobile phones have made it easier for workers to disseminate information about deaths," labor researcher Liu Kaiming tells *Time* magazine.

Western media are routinely appalled by the horrific working conditions in China. Meanwhile, Chinese media are routinely shocked by the horrific exploitation of Chinese workers by foreign companies.

Dubai inaugurates Burj Khalifa, the world's tallest building at 2,717 feet.

The building is named after UAE president and leader of Abu Dhabi Khalifa bin Zayed Al Nahyan, who bailed out Dubai from its unmanageable debt just a few weeks before the completion of the building.

In the latest sign of the "real estate bonanza" that partially triggered the financial crisis in 2007, the metal and glass building costs a whopping $20bn.

In practical terms, Abu Dhabi pays the bill because Dubai has run out of money to finance its debt.

Dubai World, the Dubai's state conglomerate, could not repay a $4.1bn bond issued years before; Abu Dhabi stepped in and helped them avoid default with a $10bn bailout.

Months after the opening of Burj Khalifa, the vast majority of office spaces and apartments remain empty.

The Icelandic government calls a referendum on whether the country should repay British and Dutch depositors for assets lost by Icelandic bank branches in the financial crisis.

People vote no because they don't feel compelled to pay debts accumulated by fraudulent banks.

The Icelandic volcano Eyafjallajökull erupts. The ashes spread over a vast area and cover the skies of Europe for weeks.

Nearly all flights in Europe are cancelled. The International Air Transport Association estimates the airline industry loses $200m a day.

In six days, 95,000 flights are cancelled across Europe.

Polish President Lech Kaczynski and scores of other Polish senior figures die in an airplane crash in Russia, causing a crisis in Poland.

In evaluating the Latin American response to the financial crisis, the OECD remarks how good the management of fiscal and monetary policies has been. Latin America experiences a very quick recovery.

The Latin American currency SUCRE is introduced as a virtual currency.

SUCRE replaces the US dollar in transactions between the countries of the Bolivarian Alliance for the Americas (ALBA).

The principal countries within ALBA are Venezuela, Bolivia, Ecuador, Nicaragua, and Cuba.

The OECD highlights the improved regulation and supervision of the banking sector in emerging economies and sees prospects for growth.

Dilma Rousseff wins the Brazilian presidential election by promising to continue outgoing president Lula's policies.

Although the US demand for commodities falls, China's sustained demand drives up prices. Oil resumes its pre-crisis prices.

On the Louisiana coast of the Gulf of Mexico, BP oil platform Deepwater Horizon explodes.

BP, formerly called British Petroleum, does not know how to repair the hole at the bottom of the ocean from which oil is spewing.

It is considered the world's largest oil disaster in marine waters. As 4.9m barrels of oil leak into the Gulf of Mexico, US authorities close 36% of the local fishing area.

The leak stops only months later. In just five years, the inhabitants of Louisiana have suffered the horrors of Katrina and now the largest oil spill in history.

Shares of BP drop dramatically and customers boycott its stations.

Damages are estimated to be in the billions of dollars and nobody knows when fishing will resume. BP is temporarily banned from operating in the Gulf of Mexico.

Online poker, one of the big new businesses of the decade, keeps growing.

Christiansen Capital Advisors estimates that, in 2001, consumers spent $3bn gambling online. In 2010, they spend over $24bn.

President Obama, reviewing two years of TARP, declares, "The markets are now stabilized."

The US government is able to recover much of the funds invested in TARP.

Losses are down from $66bn at the start of the year to $25bn toward the end, as banks start to pay back the emergency loans.

The Obama administration proposes to limit the percentage of banks' deposits they may use to trade and invest, commonly known as "proprietary trading."

This legislation is dubbed the "Volcker Rule," for Paul Volcker, chair of the President's Economic Recovery Advisory Board, who first proposes it.

The Dodd-Frank Wall Street Act, which aims to improve transparency and accountability in the financial system and includes the Volcker Rule, is enacted. The original draft contains tough measures but is later revised during its discussion in Congress.

Wall Street continues to spend. "Wallets Out, Wall Street Dares to Indulge," reads a *New York Times* headline.

The International Labor Organization (ILO) reports that since 2007, 27.6m more people are unemployed.

The EU and the United States have particularly high rates of unemployment.

In 2010, youth unemployment in the EU reaches 19.7%, while in the US it reaches 18%.

A UN report on the world economic situation notes, "In developed and developing countries alike, an increasing number of new college graduates continues to face enormous difficulties in finding jobs."

The ILO also estimates that 39% of the workforce lives below the poverty line, earning less than $2 a day. This is about 1.2bn people worldwide.

In a joint report, the UN Economic Commission for Africa and the African Union conclude that the global economic crisis continues to have a negative impact on African economies.

With economic growth falling to 1.6% in 2009 and export volumes falling, Africa's ability to develop and provide needed social services is endangered.

Haiti, among the poorest nations of the world, is shaken by a massive earthquake; first estimates place the death toll at over 200,000 people.

Many Haitians lose their homes. The Dominican Republic provides relief; Icelandic, US, Chinese, and Israeli rescue teams are the first to arrive.

At the end of February, another earthquake, one of the largest ever recorded, strikes Chile.

Months later, the world's attention is directed toward 33 miners trapped underground in Chile.

Reports of how the miners are passing time and coping fill newspapers around the world. The miners are rescued after nearly three months.

Six ships sail with humanitarian aid to Gaza in an attempt to break the Israeli-Egyptian blockade. Israel seizes the ships, killing nine activists in the ensuing scuffle.

Turkish Prime Minister Recep Tayyip Erdoğan calls the action "state terrorism." The UN Human Rights Council launches an independent investigation.

Faced with mounting international pressure, Israel agrees to ease the blockade.

Tension rises in the Korean peninsula after a South Korean vessel sinks in the Yellow Sea. North Korea denies any wrongdoing, but investigations points to Pyongyang as the perpetrator.

The tension mounts even more when North Korea starts shelling a disputed island on the west coast of Korea.

The shelling happens just before the year's second joint military exercise between South Korea and the US begins.

The US and Vietnam also stage joint naval activities in the South China Sea, a sign of Washington's increased interest in the area.

Asia Pacific is at the center of tensions due to its strategic value. In the Diaoyu/Senkaku Islands, a Chinese "fishing boat" is taken into custody by Japanese naval forces.

These islands are a cause of dispute for China, Taiwan, and Japan, which all claim the territory.

In New York, plans build an Islamic community center near Ground Zero stir opposition.

"It feels like a stab in the heart to, collectively, Americans, who still have that lingering pain from 9/11," says Sarah Palin, unable to distinguish between terrorism and Islam.

Leading up to the 2010 Congressional elections, a new force emerges in US politics: the Tea Party Movement, also called the Taxes Enough Already Movement.

The movement lacks any formal leader but several prominent Republicans, including the 2008 vice presidential candidate Sarah Palin, offer guidance.

With high-pitched rhetoric, the Tea Party uses all media available, including Facebook and Twitter, to spread the message of lower taxes.

In the midterm elections, Obama's Democratic Party is defeated. Republicans take the majority in the House in the largest seat change since 1968.

Nancy Pelosi steps down as Speaker of the House of Representatives in favor of John Boehner.

Political analysts argue that economic difficulties and an intolerably high unemployment rate are the root causes of the election results.

In Thailand, the "Red Shirts" take to the streets to call for general elections, but the government that took power in 2008 through a "judicial coup" won't budge.

After two months of protests and clashes, the military cracks down on the protesters.

"Soldiers shot wildly at anyone that moved. . . . Many people died because medics and ambulances were not allowed to enter Wat Pathum until almost midnight," writes one protester.

Facebook and Twitter are key sources for news reporters who want the latest updates from the upheaval in Thailand. Both sides of the conflict tweet their side of the story.

Thaksin Shinawatra, the former prime minister who had been exiled from the country, is able to inspire the Red Shirts via a video link.

After evaluating the incident, Human Rights Watch determines that the high death toll and injuries result from excessive and unnecessary use of force from security forces.

WikiLeaks reveals a video of US Apache helicopters shooting wildly at people on the streets of Baghdad. Among those shot at are two Reuters cameramen.

A 22-year-old intelligence analyst named Bradley Manning is arrested for leaking the video.

Operation Iraqi Freedom ends with the last of the United States brigade combat teams crossing the border to Kuwait.

WikiLeaks releases the Iraq War Logs, leaking over 390,000 previously secret US military reports. The Iraq War Logs paint a grim picture of the US legacy in Iraq.

The logs show how soldiers, insurgents, foreign aid workers, private contractors, and, above all, the Iraqi people fell victim to "asymmetric warfare." They detail torture, summary executions, and other war crimes.

The US authorities failed to investigate hundreds of reports of abuse, torture, rape, and even murder by Iraqi police and soldiers, whose conduct appears to be systematic and normally unpunished.

Medical reports of detainees describe prisoners shackled, blind-
folded, and hung by wrists or ankles, subjected to whipping,
punching, kicking, or electric shocks.

Tony Blair is forced to defend his decision to go to war in Iraq to
the British Parliament. The parliamentary scrutiny is triggered
by the pressure coming from families of those deceased in the
war.

WikiLeaks' campaign of leaking continues undisturbed. Human
rights lawyers in the US plan to use the material in court against
the US and British governments.

In conjunction with the Iraq War Logs, WikiLeaks also unveils
over 90,000 documents on the US-led war in Afghanistan.

The logs reveal that a secret "black" unit of the Special Forces
hunts down Taliban leaders for "kill or capture" operations without trial.

Incidents of allied troops shooting up buses and mortaring a
wedding are also included in the logs.

"Never before has it been possible to compare the reality on the
battlefield in such a detailed manner with what the US Army propaganda machinery is propagating," *Der Spiegel* writes.

The Pentagon worries about the possible implications and condemns the leaks because they "could very well get our troops and
those they are fighting with killed."

WikiLeaks' spokesperson Julian Assange announces the inten-
tion of his organization to continue to leak information. The
following round of leaks involves American diplomatic cables.

In total, 250,000 diplomatic documents are given to select newspapers to be published. They reveal the raw truth about US foreign policy and its two-faced operations.

The cache of cables "provides an unprecedented look at backroom bargaining by embassies around the world, brutally candid views of foreign leaders, and frank assessments of nuclear and terrorist threats," writes the *New York Times*.

The WikiLeaks website is attacked by flooding its servers with traffic, thereby making it inaccessible.

After a visit to Sweden, two women file charges against Julian Assange, alleging rape and sexual abuses.

Fearing that he could be turned over to US authorities, Assange hands himself over to British police. Hundreds of supporters attend his hearings in London.

Facebook is valued at $41bn, the third largest US Internet company after Google and Amazon.

Downloads to Amazon's ebook reader, the Kindle, surpass the company's sales of both hardcover and paperback books.

Apple unveils its latest device: the iPad, a tablet computer based on the previous and still highly successful iPhone technology. Apple sells 300,000 iPads on the first day.

The number of African mobile-phone subscribers goes from zero a little more than a decade ago to 506m, and they are expected to total 800m by 2014, according to industry analyst Informa Telecoms & Media.

Netflix, a provider of on-demand DVDs and Internet video streaming, dominates the web's traffic. During peak hours, Netflix is responsible for 20% of US Internet traffic. Its customer base exceeds 10m users.

The Burmese authorities finally release Aung San Suu Kyi from her house arrest, after being detained for 15 of the past 21 years.

The *Washington Post* reveals that the use of Special Forces to perform covert operations around the world has increased with Obama in the White House.

In 2010, Yemen receives $150m from the US for "security assistance," more than double what it received the previous year.

With the Nobel Peace Prize winner at the helm in the US, Special Forces are deployed in 75 countries, compared with 60 at the end of the Bush presidency.

Since entering office, president Obama has met with opposition to his campaign promise of healthcare reform. After much negotiating and compromising, a reform passes in 2010.

"This legislation will not fix everything that ails our health care system, but it moves us decisively in the right direction," comments Obama.

President Obama signs into law the repeal of the "Don't Ask, Don't Tell" policy, the 17-year-old ban on homosexuals serving openly in the US military.

The Fed decides to issue another round of quantitative easing to further stimulate economic growth.

Ben Bernanke announces the unconventional monetary policy move at the annual meeting in Jackson Hole.

The announcement triggers a bull market in the stock and futures markets. With a new round of quantitative easing, money flows into financial markets with ease and debt remains cheap.

German Economy Minister Rainer Bruederle suggests the US policy of boosting the US money supply via printing money is indirectly a currency manipulation.

This echoes the recurring US critique of China's policy of deliberately letting its currency remain undervalued.

The S&P 500, the index comprising the 500 biggest US companies, climbs 19% in four months; crude oil surges 25%.

Gold also surges 22%, signaling investors' mistrust in the dollar. Many argue that the dollar might in fact lose its reserve currency status if loose monetary policies are prolonged for too long.

The whole commodities sector surges on the back of the Fed policies with food manufacturers worried about possible escalation of prices.

Pakistan suffers the worst floods in the country's history. At least 18m people are affected.

The floods also damage wheat crops. Being the ninth largest exporter of wheat, this has a direct impact on wheat prices.

Dmitry Medvedev declares a state of emergency after bushfires threaten seven regions within Russia.

The bushfires burn much of Russian wheat crops, forcing the government to ban its export.

Together, the Pakistani floods, loose US monetary policy, and the Russian export ban cause the price of wheat and other commodities to skyrocket.

"In the last few weeks there have been signs we are heading the same way as in 2008," says Abdolreza Abbassian of the UN Food and Agricultural Organization, voicing concern for the possible beginning of a new food crisis.

Food riots explode in Mozambique and they "can be repeated anywhere in the coming years," according to Devinder Sharma, a leading Indian food analyst.

Nomura, the financial and industrial Japanese conglomerate, lists 25 countries where a food crisis could produce protests. Among them are Tunisia, Libya, Egypt, Algeria, and Morocco.

2011
At a Glance

World GDP: $70.01tn (numbers estimated by IMF)
  US: $15.06tn (estimated)
  China: $6.99tn (estimated)
  India: $5.85tn (estimated)

World population: 7bn (as of October 31)

Natural disasters:
  Over 60 die in an earthquake in Christchurch, New Zealand
  Over 15,000 die, thousands remain missing, in an earthquake and tsunami in Japan
  Over 600 die in a series of earthquakes in Turkey
  Hundreds die from tornados in several US states
  44 die, 4 million left without power in the eastern US after Hurrican Irene
  Hundreds die in the US as the Mississippi River floods

US federal debt: $14.97tn (as of August 4)
US unemployment: 9.0%

Average oil price: $108 per barrel (estimated)
Annual food price index (2002–2004=100): 230.2 (as of November)

World military spending: Not yet available
  Top spender: Not yet available
  Second spender: Not yet available
  Third spender: Not yet available

US share of total military spending: Not yet available

Time magazine person of the year: Not yet available

Nobel Peace Prize winners: Ellen Johnson Sirleaf, Leymah Gbowee, and Tawakkol Karman "for their non-violent struggle for the safety of women and for women's rights to full participation in peace-building work."

Introduction

What started as a quarrel between a frustrated fruit vendor in Tunisia and a policewoman turns into a pan-Arabic revolt, so strong as to force long-term dictators to step down. The revolution becomes a virus that spreads all over the Mediterranean basin and threatens to infect the heart of the EU: Brussels. In the United States, the Occupy Wall Street movement starts with peaceful protests in New York City and quickly spreads to hundreds of cities around the country and the world.

The revolution is fast, the contagion quick; it all happens at the speed of Twitter.

Amid dealing with a failing economy, Japan is hit by a 9.0 magnitude earthquake that triggers a tsunami.

The tsunami devastates the east coast of the island of Honshu, killing 15,000 people while 10,000 more are missing. The waves destroy whatever buildings they come across.

Millions of people watch shocking videos of the devastation on YouTube and use Twitter to communicate with the victims.

After the earthquake and the tsunami, reports of trouble at the Fukushima nuclear power plant start to circulate.

Tepco, the Japanese company that owns the power plant, is slow to address the international community's concerns about the Fukushima plant.

International newspapers report that, in the past, Tepco has been criticized for security breaches. It appears the earthquake and tsunami have damaged the plant's cooling system.

With very slow and often counter-productive communication, the CEO of Tepco acknowledges that the cooling system of the six reactors may have been damaged.

The plant was protected by a seawall, which did not withstand the 46-foot-high tsunami.

People film and post online three explosions happening at the first three reactors. The world is shocked and worried.

Stories of devastation and fear of what might happen fill the news. Radiation levels rise almost daily until they reach the same level as those of Chernobyl.

Embassies from all over the world instruct their citizens to leave the area; some also suggest they avoid Tokyo, which could be hit by a "radioactive wind."

The radiation coming from the Fukushima nuclear plant contaminates the sea; food cultivated in the area is banned from sale.

Many governments from all over the world announce they will scale down their nuclear plants.

Many accuse the Japanese government of having underestimated the troubles at the Tepco nuclear plant.

Thousands of people donate money to Japan in an effort to mitigate the devastating impact of the two disasters.

In a matter of days, roads are reopened and life goes back to normal, though the Japanese economy, already suffering, is crippled.

Worries of a double-dip crisis resurface globally as inflation rises while economic growth still lags behind.

The UK economy, growing at a reasonable rate in 2010, begins slowing down again in the first quarter of 2011.

Food and energy prices rise exponentially. The rise in commodity prices, which had been a feature of the pre-crisis in 2007, fuels inflation.

Commodity prices rise even more because the Fed's loose monetary policy is weakening the USD, the currency used in all commodities transactions.

Wheat, corn, and cotton reach all-time highs.

Russia and the Ivory Coast impose export bans, which further drive up prices of wheat and cocoa respectively. The price of oil surges over $100 a barrel.

Stagflation, the so-called two-headed monster where inflation rises with no economic growth, looms in the background.

Protests start to mount in Tunisia and Algeria. People take to the street to voice their anger against corrupt administrations and the rise in the cost of living.

The protests were sparked by the self-burning by Mohamed Bouazizi, a Tunisian fruit vendor. He set fire to himself after being harassed by officials.

The protests spread rapidly, reaching from Morocco to Iraq and beyond. Citizens rise up to their oppressors and demand civil liberties and an end to corruption.

Hesitant to support the protestors, the Western world stammers at press conferences. The leaders Ben Ali of Tunisia and Hosni Mubarak of Egypt had guaranteed support in the US war on terror.

After weeks of protest, Ben Ali, president of Tunisia for 24 years, resigns and flees to Saudi Arabia.

It soon emerges that French Foreign Minister Michèle Alliot-Marie has offered help to the Tunisian regime to quell the uprising.

Her family had invested heavily in real estate in Tunisia thanks to their strong ties with Ben Ali.

When the press reveals that she has used the private jet of close associates of Ben Ali while on vacation in Tunisia, Alliot-Marie is forced to resign.

Revolts break out in Egypt, one of the largest consumers of wheat in the world.

Frustration about rising food prices and anger toward political leaders becomes an explosive cocktail in Cairo.

The Egyptian military, composed of drafted soldiers, soon joins the protests. In other countries, like Syria and Libya, the professional army turn their guns on protesters.

Facebook and Twitter are instrumental in what becomes known as the Arab Spring. People bypass the official censored media using these instruments of social media.

Gus O'Donnell, the UK cabinet secretary, says that the Internet has "profoundly changed" the way people protest.

"While the core of rebellion was born on Facebook, it's Twitter where word really spread and organizations and opposition groups organized themselves," describes an article on citizen-journalism website BeforeItsNews.com.

After 30 years in power, Hosni Mubarak resigns from the Egyptian presidency.

As protests spread to oil-producing Libya, Western governments feel compelled to show their support for the uprising against Muammar Gaddafi, who has ruled the country for 40 years.

It will take a few weeks for France, Great Britain, and the US to obtain a UN mandate to intervene.

The UN Security Council approves a "no fly-zone," with Russia and China abstaining from the vote.

Western countries start a military mission similar to that of Kosovo; they want to make sure Gaddafi is unable to send air strikes against his own people.

The intervention starts on the anniversary of the beginning of the Iraq war and soon evolves into a "kinetic military action," attacking many other military installments.

Initially, the Arab League supports the intervention, but quickly reverses its decision and sharply criticizes the mission, joined in its criticism by China, Russia, Brazil, and India.

Libyan rebels conquer the eastern side of the country and declare a new government in Benghazi to manage relations with the world. They also create a central bank to handle oil revenues.

In a matter of weeks, Gaddafi is able to destroy most of the oil fields under rebel control. However, the tide soon turns and Gaddafi is ousted.

Several weeks later, Gaddafi is found and killed in the street near his hometown. His death is caught on a video, which spreads virally throughout the world within minutes.

In Bahrain, Saudi troops using US weapons crush people demonstrating for freedom and democracy. Western powers stay well clear of this revolt.

Protests spread throughout the Middle East, reaching Yemen, Oman, Jordan, Kuwait, Morocco, Gaza, Iraq, Iran, and Syria.

In most of these countries, the leadership dismisses cabinet ministers and promises referenda on constitutional change: a strategy to maintain power.

In Syria, violence escalates and the police and army fire on the population, massacring civilians.

The new Egyptian government brokers an agreement between Hamas and Fatah, which will now cooperate in leading the Palestinian people.

Muqtada al-Sadr returns to Iraq. He calls for Iraq's government to make sure that all US forces leave the country by the end of the year as promised.

Human Rights Watch observes that since the invasion of Iraq in 2003, women's rights have deteriorated.

Female activists in Iraq are regularly threatened and even attacked. Women trafficking and prostitution has also increased in the whole region.

"Many of these poor girls who think they are escaping their hard life in Iraq end up in Syria dancing in night clubs," says one activist.

2004 Nobel laureate Wangari Maathai dies just weeks before the Nobel Peace Prize is awarded to three women activists: Ellen Johnson Sirleaf, Leymah Gbowee, and Tawakkol Karman.

Torture continues under the new Iraqi government. It is revealed to be particularly abusive and offensive at the prison in the old Muthanna airport.

WikiLeaks releases the Guantánamo Files about Guantánamo detainees. The documents show that many are ordinary Afghans that had nothing to do with terrorism.

Failing to fulfill his election promise to close the camp and bring the terrorists to justice under civilian law, President Obama resumes military trials of terror suspects detained at Guantá-namo.

China worries that the Arab Spring may contaminate its most rebellious region in the west of the country.

China's budget for police and domestic surveillance surpasses the official budget of the military, amounting to $95bn.

Mexico spends $9bn to fund its police activities, mainly to fight the war against the drug cartels.

Marisol Valles García disappears. The 21-year-old criminology student had volunteered as police chief in a border town plagued by the ongoing drug wars in Mexico.

Americans are the main consumers of drugs produced or traf-ficked through Mexico. According to the US Department of Health and Human Services, 22m Americans use illegal drugs.

Mexican deaths linked to drug-related violence reach 34,000 people since the beginning of the war on drugs initiated by Mexi-can President Felipe Calderon in 2006.

"Gun purchases in the US are used to facilitate violence here in Mexico," declares Mexican Foreign Secretary Patricia Espinosa.

A loose collection of hackers calling themselves Anonymous threatens many large financial institutions, as well as local govern-ments like the Bay Area Rapid Transit (BART) in San Francisco and the infamous Mexican drug cartel the Zetas.

By 2011, Lady Gaga has been on the cover of almost every influ-ential music and fashion magazine.

In May 2011, she appears on the cover of *Rolling Stone* for the third time. Other prominent magazines that have run the pop diva's picture on their covers are *Vogue*, *Vanity Fair*, and *Elle*.

Jared Lee Loughner, a 22-year-old man, shoots at US Democratic Representative Gabrielle Giffords. The attack occurs while Giffords is meeting constituents outside a grocery store in Tuscon, Arizona.

Giffords survives but six people, including a judge, die in the shooting. The police arrests Loughner and charges him with crimes that could eventually lead to the death penalty.

The shooting raises concerns about the aggressive rhetoric of Tea Party supporters, including Sarah Palin, who before the shooting had "targeted" democratic areas with the crosshairs of a gun sight.

Seven months later, Giffords returns to the Capitol to cast her vote to raise the US debt ceiling.

Southern Sudan holds a referendum to become independent. Nearly 99% of the votes favor the proposal.

China, a major partner of Sudan, promotes the vote to achieve peace in the region and to gain access to South Sudan resources.

The relationship among China, Sudan, and South Sudan improves as China promises investments in both states and assures both governments that it needs their natural resources.

"One of the most amusing aspects of international development work in the last few years has been the paranoid alarm in Western development agencies about the rising influence of China in Africa," writes the *Guardian*.

China's investment in Africa is forecast to exceed $110bn in 2011, setting a new record. China invests in many sectors, ranging from agriculture to mining and technology.

"Africa is going to be the fastest growing region in the next decade," says Stephen Jennings of Renaissance Capital, an investment bank that focuses on emerging markets.

All emerging countries trade with Africa with growing success.

China supports the Colombian government's effort to build a railroad connecting Colombia's Atlantic and Pacific coasts.

The project is called the "Dry Canal" because it will compete with the Panama Canal.

China actively pursues diplomatic involvement in Latin America. It establishes trade agreements with all major economies and its trade volume booms.

China surpasses the US as Brazil's major trading partner, and President Dilma Rousseff says she would prioritize her country's ties with China.

According to Reuters, however, Brazil is "naïve in its relationship with China." Brasilia wants to get the most out of its relationship with Beijing, but also seeks to benefit from trading with the US.

This policy seems successful: the country grows steadily and in January its unemployment rate reaches a ten-year low.

According to the International Labor Organization, Brazil's fast development is due to a mix of policies that achieve high levels of growth as well as social goals.

"We have the perception that America is the center of everything, but we are beginning to realize that America is not the center of everything, and it hasn't been for many years," says Russell Napier, a stock market historian, in an interview to the *Financial Times*.

"For the last 10 years emerging markets have been actually driving the world," he continues.

Robert Rubin, a former US treasury secretary, sounds the alarm about the debt position of the US.

"There is a risk of disruption to [US] bond and currency markets from the fear of much higher interest rates due to future imbalances or from fear of inflation because of efforts to monetize [US] debt," Rubin speculates.

Overall, investors become slowly but inexorably bearish on the dollar, selling vast quantities and making the value of the greenback plummet.

China, the biggest lender to the US, starts to diversify its portfolio and to voice its concerns about the management of US debt.

The US government is just hours away from having to shut down all government activity when Congress fails to pass the budget in time.

The US hits its $14.3 trillion debt ceiling.

The government is forced to withdraw money from pension and disability funds to keep working until Congress raises the ceiling, making it possible for the US to further increase its debt.

A US default becomes a possibility when US credit default swaps, financial instruments that insure against the default of a country, are priced higher than those of Colombia, Panama, or Malaysia.

The *Financial Times* says the US defaulting on its debt is "no longer unthinkable."

"The age of America ends in 2016," reads the headline of the *Daily Mail* when the IMF quietly releases a report projecting that Chinese GDP would surpass the US by 2016.

In New York, a group of protesters set up camp in Zucotti Park under the banner Occupy Wall Street. They claim to stand for the 99% of Americans who have not seen their income grow as drastically as the top 1%.

Within weeks, Occupy movements sprout up in many major cities across the United States. Others join protests in cities across Europe as well. The protesters are met with police violence in some cities, catapulting them into the news media.

Standard & Poor's downgrades the US from AAA status. This, coupled with the euro crisis centered in Italy, sends the markets into a downward spiral.

The managing director of the IMF, Dominique Strauss-Kahn, is charged with raping and sexually assaulting a hotel maid at the Sofitel in New York.

Police stop him at JFK airport in New York before his Air France flight to Paris departs.

After a few days, Strauss-Kahn is placed under house arrest while the details of the case are examined.

The race for his successor as the head of the IMF starts with emerging economies voicing their concerns about another European head of the Fund.

Ministers and leading economists from Mexico, Singapore, India, and Turkey put forward their candidacy. Christine Lagarde, the French finance minister, gets the post.

Months later, all charges against Strauss-Kahn are dropped in the US. In France, another woman accuses him of sexual assault, but those charges are later dropped due to statutes of limitations.

Lagarde is one of the strongest critics of Western government reactions to the financial crisis and an advocate for tougher regulations.

Lagarde is the first woman to head the IMF and, since the IMF is deeply involved in the European debt crisis, is strongly supported by European leaders.

As the sovereign debt crisis in Europe continues, it seems that the age of Western supremacy is ending faster than expected.

"Europe could potentially fall apart," says George Soros, the billionaire investor, at a meeting in Davos, Switzerland.

Nouriel Roubini, the economist known for having predicted the 2007 financial crisis, states, "What's happening in the Eurozone is certainly one of the biggest risks to the global economy."

Greece faces a financial crisis that could lead to insolvency and is offered a bailout by the European Union in exchange for harsh austerity measures.

Greek Prime Minister Papandreou offers to step down in favor of a new unity government. Talk of leaving the euro sends global markets into a panic.

Financial markets shift their attention to Italy where lack of political commitment, mounting debt and rising interest rates put the country in a similar position to that of Greece. In Brussels and elsewhere, the idea that if Italy falls the EU would collapse spreads.

In a matter of three months yields on ten year Italian government bonds rise over 7% and the spread to the German bund fluctuates north of 500 points.

Pressured by financial markets and European leaders, the Italian premier, Silvio Berlusconi, resigns. After a decade long campaign against the Italian premier, the Economist headlines "The end of Berlusconi. Halleluiah".

The newly formed Italian government is headed by Mario Monti, a distinguished professor who forms a team of academics to reform Italy, face the mounting debt and get the Italian economy growing.

However, at the end of the year both the IMF and the OECD believe 2012 would be a recessive year in Italy.

The German economy, widely regarded as the powertrain of Europe, starts to slow down and by the end of November the price of refinancing debt for all European economies rise.

Kevin Gaynor, strategist at Nomura, a major Japanese industrial and financial conglomerate, argues that the Great Recession of 2007-2009 did not start with the subprime financial crisis, but in 2001 when the Fed forced rates to their lowest levels.

Gaynor comes to the conclusion that fundamental changes in 2001 have greatly shaped the rest of the decade.

Osama bin Laden is shot dead in a raid carried out by US Navy Seals in Abbottabad, Pakistan, without prior knowledge by the Pakistani authorities.

His body is buried at sea. Bin Laden has become an icon; few believe that his death will change the situation in Iraq or Afghanistan.

"Justice is done," says President Obama on the evening of May 1, 2011. People take to the streets to celebrate while the world watches in astonishment.

Outside the US, the execution raises questions of breeches of international law by the US.

By 2011, Osama bin Laden is merely a symbol. The current movement for better governments in the Arab world is already on its way, looking to topple the near enemies: corrupt oligarchic Muslim elites.

"Africa is the Silicon Valley of banking," says Carol Realini, executive chair of Obopay, a California-based mobile-banking innovator.

"The future of banking is being defined here. The new models for what will be mainstream throughout the world are being incubated here. It's going to change the world," she continues.

The major innovation introduced in Africa is mobile banking. Although it is available in Japan and other countries, mobile banking is huge in Africa.

Safaricom was launched in 2007 in Kenya. Its main product is a money-transfer-by-text-message called M-Pesa. Today 12m people in Kenya use M-Pesa, in a country of 39m people.

Miramax signs an agreement with Netflix, an online streaming service worth at least $100m. Netflix members can watch an unlimited number of movies and TV-series online for a monthly fee.

The G8 in Paris is defined as the G8 of super-debt, as most nations run unmanageable budget deficits.

A scandal breaks out over *News of the World* reporters allegedly hacking into voicemails of government officials, police officers, and the general public in their pursuit of news. Several executives resign.

Sean Hoare, the former *News of the World* journalist who first revealed that the phone hacking was "endemic" is found dead. The police conclude that it was a suicide.

AOL purchases the Huffington Post, "one of the most heavily visited news Web sites in the [United States]," according to the *New York Times*. Arianna Huffington, its founder, takes over all of AOL's editorial content as president and editor-in-chief of its new media arm.

Steve Jobs, iconic co-founder and former CEO of Apple, dies of pancreatic cancer.

Vigils are held throughout the world. A quote from a speech he gave in 2005 makes the rounds on Facebook and Twitter, in newspapers and magazines, on websites and television: "Remembering that you are going to die is the best way I know to avoid the trap of thinking you have something to lose.... There is no reason not to follow your heart."

On July 22, a fertilizer bomb, similar to the one Timothy McVeigh exploded in Oklahoma, explodes in front of the Cabinet offices in Oslo, Norway.

It causes great damage to the city center, including the prime minister's office. Eight people die in the blast.

Soon afterwards, a Christian fundamentalist on a self-proclaimed crusade against Islam and those who support a multicultural society, steps ashore on the little island of Utøya, near Oslo.

Anders Behring Breivik's opinions coincide with mainstream right-wing extremist groups across Europe. He claims to have had assistance from people in all major European countries and the US.

Hundreds of youths are attending the Labor party's traditional youth summer camp on the island.

Armed with dum-dum bullets designed to explode inside the body, Behring Breivik, dressed as a police officer, tells the youths to gather round as he has information about the Oslo bombing.

Then he shoots them one by one. He shoots fleeing children in the back and shoots those he can find hiding in bushes and cliffs. At least 68 youths are confirmed dead.

Having pleaded not guilty, he remains in custody awaiting trial.

Behring Breivik had written an extensive manifesto explaining his ambition to drive Muslims out of Europe and to hurt the Labor party beyond recovery.

In his manifesto, he details nearly 10 years of planning his mass murder.

Afterword

THIS WAS THE DECADE of people's empowerment, when civil society was handed new digital tools to make its voice heard.

Social media gave people the arena, and technology gave them the tools to report their own news in real time to a global audience. Gone are the corporate filters or government censorship, gone is the propaganda that led to the invasion of Iraq, and gone is the use of violence to protest. Today, images from YouTube are stronger than any weapons; reports of power abuses and calls to protest travel as fast as the wind on the wings of Twitter—nobody can stop them!

In the aftermath of the Arab Spring, Tunisia and Egypt face the challenge of nation building, while people are still protesting in other parts of the Arab world. This is a movement Western leaders find difficult to support as it topples dictators they have backed for decades. This is a movement that also exposes the hypocrisy of the West, which until yesterday was doing business with brutal dictators like Gaddafi.

Social media are exposing these double standards. WikiLeaks documents have unveiled the degree of Western leaders' deceit: we now have access to what they say to each other behind closed doors.

At the beginning of the millennium, the US, the winner of

the Cold war, was a beacon of light, of democracy and free-dom. Today, the faith and trust in the US as a role model have all but vanished. Globalization has empowered emerging economies at the periphery of the Western empire, opening young people's eyes to new places like Rio de Janeiro or Beijing to pursue their fortune and happiness. The world is no longer divided into a North and a South, or an East and a West. It has grown more complex, more exciting, and it's all just a click away.

In the Far East, the transformation of China into an economic superpower simultaneously gives hope and instills fear in different corners of the world. In African countries, Chinese companies are generally a welcome source of investments not tainted by the history of atrocities, oppression, and lies that have characterized Western countries and companies. Politicians in the West, however, fear for their supremacy, preparing for coming conflicts with the new economic giants.

In South America, leaders like Lula and Kirchner have stirred real hope for a changed government and cooperation within Latin America, initiating a shift away from US-centered policies and toward intracontinental cooperation. Emerging from the bankruptcy and economic crisis of the 1990s, these countries are developing a new economic model.

In Europe, the power elite formed a closer, and currently financially strained, colossus of a union; its core, the euro, is now falling apart. Against this backdrop, the Arab Spring has contaminated Europe.

Despite a tenure of broken promises, Obama will forever be

remembered as the president who caught Osama bin Laden. But when he did, it was already yesterday's story. The story of the day was the movement for freedom, justice, and democracy, which is being written digitally, away from America: in North Africa, in the Middle East, and in European squares.

As the second decade of the new millennium begins, the digital lifestyle has become a reality, empowering people and frustrating politicians. The decade of deceit, when transparent government was sacrificed on the altar of fake security and partisan politics, ends with the uncontested victory of the technological revolution that empowers the people.

References

2001

"National Academy of Sciences Affirms IPCC Findings Panel Tells Bush Global Warming is Getting Worse." *New York Times*, June 7, 2001.

Stockholm International Peace Research Institute (SIPRI). *SIPRI Yearbook 2002: Armaments, Disarmament and International Security*. Oxford: Oxford University Press, 2002.

2002

Associated Press. "London March Against Iraq War Draws 150,000." *Baltimore Sun,* September 29, 2002. http://www.baltimoresun.com/bal-te.britian29sep29,0,4581504.story.

BBC. "Excerpts: Saddam Hussein's Letter." September 20, 2002, http://news.bbc.co.uk/2/hi/middle_east/2270520.stm.

Davis, Patty. "US Rejects International Criminal Court Treaty." CNN, May 6, 2002. http://articles.cnn.com/2002-05-06/justice/international.court_1_international-criminal-court-treaty-crimes-defense-secretary-donald-rumsfeld?_s=PM:LAW.

Diamond, John. "Rumsfeld OK'd Harsh Treatment." *USA Today*. June 22, 2004. http://www.usatoday.com/news/washington/2004-06-22-rumsfeld-abuse-usat_x.htm.

Feeney, Mark. "Abuse in the Catholic Church." *Boston Globe*, April 8, 2003. http://www.boston.com/globe/spotlight/abuse/extras/pulitzers.htm.

Kawach, Nadin. "War Threat Against Iraq Unethical, Scott Ritter." Al-Jazeera, March 2, 2003. http://www.aljazeerah.info/News%20archives/2003%20News%20archives/March%202003%20News/Aljazeerah,%20News,%20March%202,%202003/Scott%20Ritter,%20war%20on%20Iraq%20unethical%20News%20March%202,%202003%20www.aljazeerah.info.htm.

New York Times. "Quotation of the Day." September 7, 2002, http://www.nytimes.com/2002/09/07/nyregion/quotation-of-the-day-766518.html.

SIPRI. *SIPRI Yearbook 2003*. Oxford: Oxford University Press, 2003.

Taylor, Matthew. "David Kelly Postmortem Reveals Injuries Were Self-Inflicted." *Guardian*, October 22, 2010. http://www.guardian.co.uk/politics/2010/oct/22/david-kelly-postmortem-self-inflicted.

2003

BBC. "Millions Join Global Anti-War Protests." February 17, 2003, http://news.bbc.co.uk/2/hi/europe/2765215.stm.

———. "Parmalat to sue Bank of America." October 7, 2004, http://news.bbc.co.uk/2/hi/business/3724540.stm.

Bumiller, Elisabeth. "Bush's Tutor and Disciple—Condoleezza Rice." *New York Times*, November 17, 2004. http://www.nytimes.com/2004/11/17/politics/17rice.html?_r=1.

CNN. "CNN Late Edition With Wolf Blitzer." March 9, 2003, http://archives.cnn.com/TRANSCRIPTS/0303/09/le.00.html.

———. "Rockets Hit Two Hotels in Baghdad." November 21, 2003, http://articles.cnn.com/2003-11-20/world/sprj.irq.main_1_convoy-iraqi-police-palestine-hotel?_s=PM:WORLD.

Coppers, Matthew, Massimo Calabresi, and John F. Dickerson. "A War on Wilson?" *TIME Magazine*, July 17, 2003. http://www.time.com/time/nation/article/0,8599,465270,00.html.

SIPRI. *SIPRI Yearbook 2004*. Oxford: Oxford University Press, 2004.

Guardian. "Full text of Colin Powell's speech." February 5, 2003, http://www.guardian.co.uk/world/2003/feb/05/iraq.usa.

Hersh, Seymour M. *Chain of Command: The Road From 9/11 to Abu Ghraib*. New York: HarperCollins, 2004.

———. "Who Lied to Whom?" *The New Yorker*, March 31, 2003. http://www.newyorker.com/archive/2003/03/31/030331fa_fact1.

USA Today. "Confronting Iraq: Prewar Predictions Coming Back to Bite." April 1, 2003, http://www.usatoday.com/educate/war28-article.htm.

Zucchino, David. "Army Stage-Managed Fall of Hussein Statue." *Los Angeles Times*, July 3, 2004. http://articles.latimes.com/2004/jul/03/nation/na-statue3.

2004

BBC. "UN Rules Against Israeli Barrier." July 9, 2004, http://news.bbc.co.uk/2/hi/middle_east/3879057.stm.

———. "US Attacks Belgium War Crimes Law." June 12, 2003, http://news.bbc.co.uk/2/hi/europe/2985744.stm.

Bernton, Hal. "Woman Loses Her Job Over Coffins Photo." *Seattle Times*, April 22, 2004. http://seattletimes.nwsource.com/html/localnews/2001909527_coffin22m.html.

CNN. "2 Arrested as France's Ban on Burqas, Niqabs Takes Effect." April 11, 2011, http://articles.cnn.com/2011-04-11/world/france.burqa.ban_1_france-s-islamic-burqas-french-muslim?_s=PM:WORLD.

Egeland, Jan. *A Billion Lives: An Eyewitness Report From the Frontlines of Humanity*. New York: Simon & Schuster, 2004.

Hersh, Seymour M. "Torture and Abu Ghraib." *The New Yorker*, May 10, 2004. http://www.newyorker.com/archive/2004/05/10/040510fa_fact.

Human Rights Watch. *Getting Away With Torture?* New York: Human Rights Watch, 2005.

———. *Guantanamo: Detainee Accounts*. New York: Human Rights Watch, 2004.

———. *Israel's "Separation Barrier" in the Occupied West Bank: Human Rights and International Humanitarian Law Consequences*. New York: Human Rights Watch, 2004.

———. *The United States' "Disappeared": The CIA's Long-Term "Ghost Detainees."* New York: Human Rights Watch, 2004.

McDonnell, Patrick J. "U.S. Mopping Up as Insurgents Make Last Stand in Fallujah." *Los Angeles Times*, November 17, 2004. http://articles.baltimoresun.com/2004-11-17/news/0411170341_1_marines-alpha-insurgents.

Okrent, Daniel. "Weapons of Mass Destruction? Or Mass Distraction?" *New York Times*, May 30, 2004. http://www.nytimes.com/2004/05/30/weekinreview/the-public-editor-weapons-of-mass-destruction-or-mass-distraction.html.

SIPRI. *SIPRI Yearbook 2005*. Oxford: Oxford University Press, 2005.

2005

CNN. "US Recieves Aid Offers From Around the World." September 4, 2005, http://edition.cnn.com/2005/US/09/04/katrina.world.aid/.

The Economist. "Special Report on the Future of Finance." January 24, 2009, http://www.economist.com/node/12957709.

Faiola, Anthony. "N. Korea Declares Itself a Nuclear Power." *Washington Post*, February 10, 2005. http://www.washingtonpost.com/wp-dyn/articles/A12836-2005Feb10.html.

Gerth, Jeff and Scott Shane. "US is Said to Pay to Plant Articles in Iraq Papers." *New York Times*, December 1, 2005. http://www.nytimes.com/2005/12/01/politics/01propaganda.html.

Glover, Julian. "Two-Thirds Believe London Bombings Are Linked to Iraq War." *Guardian*, July 19, 2005. http://www.guardian.co.uk/uk/2005/jul/19/iraq.july7.

O'Brien, Keith and Bryan Bender. "Chronology of Errors: how a disaster spread." *Boston Globe*, September 11, 2005. http://www.boston.com/news/weather/articles/2005/09/11/chronology_of_errors_how_a_disaster_spread/.

OECD. *The Economic Impact of Counterfeiting and Piracy*. Paris: OECD, 2005.

Raghuram, Rajan G. "Has Financial Development Made the World Riskier?" Proceedings, Federal Reserve Bank of Kansas City, issue Aug. (2005): 313-369.

Sgrena, Giuliana. *Friendly Fire: The Remarkable Story of a Journalist Kidnapped in Iraq, Rescued by an Italian Secret Service Agent, and Shot by US Forces.* Chicago: Haymarket Books, 2006.

SIPRI. *SIPRI Yearbook 2006.* Oxford: Oxford University Press, 2006.

White, Ben. "Chinese Drop Bid to Buy US Oil Firm." *Washington Post,* August 3, 2005. http://www.washingtonpost.com/wp-dyn/content/article/2005/08/02/AR2005080200404.html.

World Health Organization. *WHO Air Quality Guidelines for Particulate Matter, Ozone, Nitrogen Dioxide and Sulfur Dioxide.* Geneva: World Health Organization, 2005.

2006

"06CAIRO493." WikiLeaks. http://wikileaks.org/cable/2006/01/06CAIRO493.html.

Akerlof, George A. and Robert J. Shiller. *Animal Spirits: How Human Psychology Drives the Economy, and Why It Matters for Global Capitalism.* Princeton: Princeton University Press, 2009.

BBC. "General Seeks UK Iraq Withdrawl." October 13, 2006, http://news.bbc.co.uk/2/hi/6046332.stm.

———. "Pope's Speech Stirs Muslim Anger." September 14, 2006, http://news.bbc.co.uk/2/hi/5346480.stm.

Destrebecq, Denis. *Cocaine Trafficking in Western Africa: Situation Report.* Vienna: UNODC, 2007.

"The Euro at Ten: Lessons and Challenges." Fifth ECB Central Banking Conference, Frankfurt, November 13–14, 2008.

"FBI Director Mueller's Visit to Egypt REF: Cairo 493." WikiLeaks. http://wikileaks.org/cable/2006/02/06CAIRO941.html.

Human Rights Watch. *Fatal Strikes.* New York: Human Rights Watch, 2006.

———. *Sweden Violated Torture Ban in CIA Rendition.* New York: Human Rights Watch, 2006.

Lane, Charles. "High Court Rejects Detainee Tribunals." *Washington Post,* June 30, 2006. http://www.washingtonpost.com/wp-dyn/content/article/2006/06/29/AR2006062900928.html.

SIPRI. *SIPRI Yearbook 2007.* Oxford: Oxford University Press, 2007.

2007

The Age. "APEC Climate Agreement a 'Diplomatic Breakthrough.'" September 9, 2007, http://www.theage.com.au/news/national/downer-hails-climate-deal/2007/09/09/1189276521977.html.

Bank for International Settlements. *79th Annual Report.* Basel, Switzerland: BIS, 2009.

Burns, John F. and Alissa J. Rubin. "U.S. Arming Sunnis in Iraq to Battle Old Qaeda Allies." *New York Times,* June 11, 2007. http://www.nytimes.com/2007/06/11/world/middleeast/11iraq.html?pagewanted=print.

CBS. "Suicide Epidemic Among Veterans." February 11, 2007, http://www.cbsnews.com/stories/2007/11/13/cbsnews_investigates/main3496471.shtml?tag=contentMain;contentBody.

European Parliament. *Temporary Committee on the Alleged Use of European Countries by the CIA for the Transport and Illegal Detention of Prisoners.* Working Document No. 9, 2007.

"French Ambassador's Views on Tunisian Political." WikiLeaks. http://www.wikileaks.ch/cable/2007/08/07TUNIS1095.html.

Guardian. "FBI Abused Patriot Act Powers, Audit Finds." March 9, 2007, http://www.guardian.co.uk/world/2007/mar/09/usa.

Lai Stirland, Sarah, "'Open-Source Politics' Taps Facebook for Myanmar Protests." *Wired,* October 4, 2007. http://www.wired.com/politics/onlinerights/news/2007/10/myanmarfacebook.

Langer, Gary. "Voices from Iraq 2007: Ebbing Hope in a Landscape of Loss." ABC News, March 19, 2007. http://abcnews.go.com/US/story?id=2954716&page=1.

New York Times. "A Glimpse Into the CIA's 'Family Jewels.'" June 26, 2007, http://www.nytimes.com/2007/06/26/world/americas/26iht-cia.5.6349602.html.

OECD. *Economic Survey of India, 2007.* Paris: OECD, 2007.

——. *OECD Factbook 2007: Economic, Environmental and Social Statistics.* Paris: OECD, 2007.

Reid, Tim. "Iran Halted Its Nuclear Weapons Programme in 2003, US Agencies Say." *The Sunday Times,* December 4, 2007. http://www.timesonline.co.uk/tol/news/world/us_and_americas/article2995111.ece.

Rice, Xan. "China's Economic Invasion of Africa." *Guardian,* February 6, 2011. http://www.guardian.co.uk/world/2011/feb/06/chinas-economic-invasion-of-africa.

SIPRI. *SIPRI Yearbook 2008.* Oxford: Oxford University Press, 2008.

Solomon, S., D. Qin, M. Manning, Z. Chen, M. Marquis, K. B. Averyt, M. Tignor, and H. L. Miller. *Contribution of Working Group I to the Fourth Assessment Report of the Intergovernmental Panel on Climate Change.* Cambridge: Cambridge University Press, 2007.

Taylor, Ian. *China's New Role in Africa.* Boulder, CO: Lynne Rienner Publishers Inc., 2008.

UNEP. *Post-Conflict Environmental Assessment.* Nairobi: UNEP, 2007.

Urquhart, Conal. "Israel Planned For Lebanon War Months in Advance, PM Says." *Guardian,* March 8, 2007. http://www.guardian.co.uk/world/2007/mar/09/syria.israelandthepalestinians.

2008

CNN. "Riots, Instability Spread as Food Prices Skyrocket." April 14, 2008, http://articles.cnn.com/2008-04-14/world/world.food.crisis_1_food-aid-food-prices-rice-prices?_s=PM:WORLD.

Eichengreen, Barry. "Thoughts About the Subprime Crisis." Economia Politica, 2008.

Hari, Johann. "You are Being Lied to about Pirates." *Independent*, January 5, 2009. http://www.independent.co.uk/opinion/commentators/johann-hari/johann-hari-you-are-being-lied-to-about-pirates-1225817.html.

Hersh, Seymour M. "Preparing the Battlefield." *The New Yorker*, July 7, 2008. http://www.newyorker.com/reporting/2008/07/07/080707fa_fact_hersh.

Human Rights Watch. *Locked Up Alone*. New York: Human Rights Watch, 2008.

Johnson, Simon, and James Kwak. *13 Bankers: The Wall Street Takeover and the Next Financial Meltdown*. New York: Pantheon, 2010.

Krugman, Paul. *Conscience of a Liberal: Reclaiming America from the Right*. New York: W. W. Norton & Co., 2007.

OECD. *Latin American Economic Outlook*. Paris: OECD, 2008.

"President Ben Ali Meets With A/S Welch: Progress." WikiLeaks. wikileaks.ch/cable/2008/03/08TUNIS193.html.

SIPRI. *SIPRI Yearbook 2009*. Oxford: Oxford University Press, 2009.

Stiglitz, Joseph and Linda Bilmes. *The Three Trillion Dollar War: The True Cost of the Iraq Conflict*. New York: W. W. Norton & Co., 2009.

United Nations. *World Economic Situation and Prospects 2009*. New York: UN, 2009.

2009

BBC. "Blasts Bring Carnage to Bagdhad." August 19, 2009, http://news.bbc.co.uk/2/hi/8208976.stm.

———. "UN Backs Gaza 'War Crimes' Report." October 16, 2009, http://news.bbc.co.uk/2/hi/8310754.stm.

Butt, Riazat. "Pope Claims Condoms Could Make African Aids Crisis Worse." *Guardian*, March 17, 2009. http://www.guardian.co.uk/world/2009/mar/17/pope-africa-condoms-aids.

CBS News. "Obama Has Increased Drone Attacks." February 12, 2010, http://www.cbsnews.com/stories/2010/02/12/politics/main6201484.shtml.

Chamberlain, Gethin and Mark Tran. "Sri Lankan Troops Mop Up Tamil Tigers as Leader Said to Have Died in Bunker." *Guardian*, May 17, 2009. http://www.guardian.co.uk/world/2009/may/17/tamil-surrender-sri-lanka.

Daily Telegraph. "Expenses: How MP's Expenses Became a Hot Topic." May 8, 2009, http://www.telegraph.co.uk/news/newstopics/mps-expenses/5294350/Expenses-How-MPs-expenses-became-a-hot-topic.html.

Eichengreen, Barry. "The Last Temptation of Risk." *National Interest*, April 30, 2009. http://nationalinterest.org/article/the-last-temptation-of-risk-3091.

Grossman, Lev. "Iran Protests: Twitter, the Medium of the Movement." *TIME Magazine*, June 17, 2009. http://www.time.com/time/world/article/0,8599,1905125,00.html.

Kimmelman, Michael. "An Italian City Shaken to Its Cultural Core." *New York Times*, December 23, 2009. http://www.nytimes.com/2009/12/24/arts/24abroad.html?pagewanted=all.

Macalister, Terry. "Rio's Deal With Chinalco Collapses." *Guardian*, June 4, 2009. http://www.guardian.co.uk/business/2009/jun/04/rio-tinto-chinalco-investment.

Padoa-Schioppa, Tommaso. *La Veduta Corta*. Bologna: Il Mulino, 2009.

Mail Foreign Service. "'They Walked Into A Trap': 76 Indian Soldiers Slaughtered by Maoist Rebels in 'brutal' Ambush." *Daily Mail*, April 7, 2010. http://www.dailymail.co.uk/news/article-1264119/Maoist-massacre-76-Indian-soldiers-ambushed-Naxalites.html.

Mir, Amir. "60 Drone Hits Kill 14 Al-Qaeda Men, 687 Civilians." *International News*, April 10, 2009.

Reinhart, Carmen M. and Kenneth S. Rogoff. *This Time is Different: Eight Centuries of Financial Folly*. Princeton: Princeton University Press, 2009.
Sarno, David. "The Internet Sure Loves Its Outlaws." *Los Angeles Times*, April 29, 2007. http://www.latimes.com/technology/la-ca-webscout29apr29,0,5609754.story.

SIPRI. *SIPRI Yearbook 2010*. Oxford: Oxford University Press, 2010.

"Troubled Tunisia: What Should We Do?" WikiLeaks. http://wikileaks.org/cable/2009/07/09TUNIS492.html.

White, Lawrence J. "The Credit Rating Agencies." *Journal of Economic Perspectives* 24, no. 2 (2010): 211–226.

World Bank. *China - From Poor Areas to Poor People: China's Evolving Poverty Reduction Agenda*. Washington, DC: World Bank, 2009.

2010

BBC. "Wikileaks 'Hacked Ahead of Secret US Document Release.'" November 28, 2010, http://www.bbc.co.uk/news/world-us-canada-11858637.

Craig, Susanne and Kevin Roose. "Wallets Out, Wall St. Dares to Indulge." *New York Times*, November 23, 2010. http://dealbook.nytimes.com/2010/11/23/signs-of-swagger-wallets-out-wall-st-dares-to-celebrate/.

Davies, Nick. "Afghanistan War Logs: Task Force 373 – Special Forces Hunting Top Taliban." *Guardian*, July 25, 2010. http://www.guardian.co.uk/world/2010/jul/25/task-force-373-secret-afghanistan-taliban.

DeYoung, Karen, and Greg Jaffe. "US 'Secret War' Expands Globally as Special Operations Forces Take Larger Role." *Washington Post*, June 4, 2010. http://www.washingtonpost.com/wp-dyn/content/article/2010/06/03/AR2010060304965.html.

European Union Times. "EU Industry Chief Voices Need to Block Chinese Takeovers." December 28, 2010, http://www.eutimes.net/2010/12/eu-industry-chief-voices-need-to-block-chinese-takeovers/.

Fox News. "Palin: Ground Zero Mosque 'Like a Stab in the Heart' to Americans." August 17, 2010, http://nation.foxnews.com/sarah-palin/2010/08/17/palin-ground-zero-mosque-stab-heart-americans.

Gebauer, Matthias, John Goetz, Hans Hoyng, Susanne Koelbl, Marcel Rosenbach, and Gregor Peter Schmitz. "Explosive Leaks Provide Image of War from Those Fighting It." *Der Spiegel*, July 25, 2010, http://www.spiegel.de/international/world/0,1518,708314,00.html.

"General Petraeus' Meeting With Saleh on Security." WikiLeaks. www.wikileaks.ch/cable/2010/01/10SANAA4.html.

Hosaka, Tomoko A. "China Surpasses Japan as World's No. 2 Economy." *Washington Post*, August 16, 2010. http://www.washingtonpost.com/wp-dyn/content/article/2010/08/15/AR2010081503697.html.

Human Rights Watch. *Descent into Chaos*. New York: Human Rights Watch, 2011.

International Labour Organization. *Global Employment Trends 2011: The Challenge of a Jobs Recovery*. (Geneva: International Labour Organization, 2011).

Melander, Ingrid and Harry Papachristou. "China's Wen Offers to Buy Greek Debt." Reuters, October 2, 2010. http://www.reuters.com/article/2010/10/02/us-greece-china-idUSTRE69112L20101002.

OECD. *China in the 2010s: Rebalancing Growth and Strengthening Social Safety Nets*. Paris: OECD, 2010.

Ramzy, Austin. "Chinese Factory Under Scrutiny As Suicides Mount." *TIME Magazine*, May 26, 2010. http://www.time.com/time/world/article/0,8599,1991620,00.html.

Shane, Scott and Andrew W. Lehren. "Leaked Cables Offer Raw Look at U.S. Diplomacy." *New York Times*, November 28, 2010. http://www.nytimes.com/2010/11/29/world/29cables.html.

SIPRI. *SIPRI Yearbook 2011*. Oxford: Oxford University Press, 2011.

United Nations Economic Commission For Africa, *Economic Report on Africa 2010: Promoting High-Level Sustainable Growth to Reduce Unemployment in Africa*. (Addis Ababa, Ethiopia: United Nations Economic Commission For Africa, 2010).

United Nations. *World Economic Situation and Prospects 2010: Global Outlook*. New York: United Nations, 2009.

Walker, Andrew. "G20 Summit Agrees to Reform IMF." BBC, October 23, 2010. http://www.bbc.co.uk/news/business-11612701.

2011

Buckley, Chris. "China Internal Security Spending Jumps Past Army Budget." Reuters, March 5, 2011. http://www.reuters.com/article/2011/03/05/china-unrest-idUS-TOE72400920110305.

Ewalt, David M. "Steve Jobs' 2005 Stanford Commencement Address." Forbes, October 5, 2011. http://www.forbes.com/sites/davidewalt/2011/10/05/steve-jobs-2005-stanford-commencement-address/.

Food and Agriculture Organization of the United Nations. "FAO Food Price Index." November 3, 2011. http://www.fao.org/worldfoodsituation/wfs-home/foodpricesindex/en/.

Gardner, David. "The Age of America Ends in 2016: IMF Predicts the Year China's Economy Will Surpass U.S." *Daily Mail*, April 26, 2011. http://www.dailymail.co.uk/news/article-1380486/The-Age-America-ends-2016-IMF-predicts-year-Chinas-economy-surpass-US.html.

Glennie, Jonathan. "WikiLeaks Cables: China's aid to Africa Has Strings Attached." *Guardian*, December 10, 2010. http://www.guardian.co.uk/global-development/poverty-matters/2010/dec/10/wikileaks-cables-china-aid-africa.

Human Rights Watch. *At a Crossroads: Human Rights in Iraq Eight Years After the US-Led Invasion*. New York: Human Rights Watch, 2011.

International Labour Organization Institute for Labour Studies. *Brazil: An Innovative Income-Led Strategy*. Geneva: International Labour Organization, 2011.

International Monetary Fund. World Economic Outlook Report. September 21, 2011. http://www.imf.org/external/pubs/ft/weo/2011/02/index.htm.

Montopoli, Brian and Robert Hendin. "Sarah Palin Criticized Over Gabrielle Giffords Presence on 'Target List.'" CBS, January 11, 2011. http://www.cbsnews.com/8301-503544_162-20027918-503544.html.

Peters, Jeremy W. and Verne G. Kopytoff. "Betting on News, AOL is Buying The Huffington Post." The New York Times, February 7, 2011. http://www.nytimes.com/2011/02/07/business/media/07aol.html.

US Bureau of Labor Statistics. "Labor Force Statistics from the Current Population Survey." November 4, 2011. http://www.bls.gov/cps/.

US Department of Energy. "World Crude Oil Prices." November 11, 2011. http://www.eia.gov/dnav/pet/pet_pri_wco_k_w.htm.

US Department of the Treasury, Bureau of the Public Debt. "The Debt to the Penny and Who Holds It." November 11, 2011. http://www.treasurydirect.gov/NP/BPDLogin.

About the Author

LORETTA NAPOLEONI is the author of the bestselling book *Rogue Economics: Capitalism's New Reality* (a *Publishers Weekly* Best Book 2008) and *Terror Incorporated: Tracing the Money Behind Global Terrorism*, both translated into fifteen languages. One of the world's leading experts on money laundering and terror financing, Napoleoni has worked as a correspondent and columnist for *La Stampa*, *La Repubblica*, *El País*, and *Le Monde*, and she has presented on the economics of terrorism for Google UK and TEDTalks. She teaches economics at the Judge Business School in Cambridge.

About Seven Stories Press

SEVEN STORIES PRESS is an independent book publisher based in New York City. We publish works of the imagination by such writers as Nelson Algren, Russell Banks, Octavia E. Butler, Ani DiFranco, Assia Djebar, Ariel Dorfman, Coco Fusco, Barry Gifford, Hwang Sok-yong, Lee Stringer, and Kurt Vonnegut, to name a few, together with political titles by voices of conscience, including the Boston Women's Health Collective, Noam Chomsky, Angela Y. Davis, Human Rights Watch, Derrick Jensen, Ralph Nader, Loretta Napoleoni, Gary Null, Project Censored, Barbara Seaman, Alice Walker, Gary Webb, and Howard Zinn, among many others. Seven Stories Press believes publishers have a special responsibility to defend free speech and human rights, and to celebrate the gifts of the human imagination, wherever we can. For additional information, visit www.sevenstories.com.